50 GUNS
THAT CHANGED AMERICA

AN ILLUSTRATED GUIDE

Skyhorse Publishing books may be purchased
in bulk at special discounts for sales promotion,
corporate gifts, fund-raising, or educational
purposes. Special editions can also be created to
specifications. For details, contact the Special Sales
Department, Skyhorse Publishing, 307 West 36th
Street, 11th Floor, New York, NY 10018 or
info@skyhorsepublishing.com.

www.skyhorsepublishing.com

10 9 8 7 6 5 4 3 2 1

Library of Congress Cataloging-in-Publication
Data is available on file.

Paperback ISBN: 978-1-5107-5638-0
eBook ISBN: 978-1-5107-7056-0

Printed in China

50 GUNS
THAT CHANGED AMERICA

AN ILLUSTRATED GUIDE

BRUCE WEXLER

Skyhorse Publishing

Contents

Introduction

Choosing just fifty guns that have been significant in the history and development of a nation as vibrant and varied as the United States is a tremendous challenge. It is evident that firearms have played a major role in the evolution of America from the early settlers, the War of Independence, the Civil War, the Wild West, and two World Wars. They are still significant today, mostly for survival and self defense. In many ways, the history of the United Sates parallels the progress of gun technology. Gunsmiths from Europe, especially from France and Germany, brought their skills to the New World and made weapons that were used to free the emerging nation from its Colonial rulers. The American Longrifle type of firearm was crucial in the fight for independence. The firearm skills of American citizens, who were used to owning and handling guns, were also important in the fight for freedom. Firearms had been vital to the survival of the original settlers and had enabled them to civilize their new land. The revolutionary struggle showed how the marksmanship skills of ordinary Americans greatly exceeded those of the British army. The United States constitution recognized the crucial nature of this familiarity with firearms and enshrined the right of the people to hold and bear arms so that they could protect their hard-earned liberty.

Starting from this point, the book considers other guns that were significant in American history. For example, Hall pioneered the first attempts to manufacture the ground-breaking breech-loading firearms. Development of these weapons coincided with the establishment and development of the National Armories at Harpers Ferry and Springfield. These manufacturers began to develop standardized parts and the principles of production-line assembly. These revolutionary methods were adopted by the motor industry at the beginning of the twentieth century.

Although the Civil War was a terrible time in the nation's history, it served to spur ingenuity on both sides of the conflict. Union and Confederate gunsmiths developed increasingly sophisticated weaponry in their attempt to outgun the opposition. Over this brief period, guns morphed from muzzle-loading single-shot weapons (the Model 1841 Springfield rifle, for example) to breech loading single-shot weapons (such as the Sharps rifle/carbine). These then developed into multiple-shot weapons like the revolvers produced by Smith & Wesson and Colt and the lever-action rifles of Spencer and Henry. The non-industrial South struggled to keep up with Yankee ingenuity. The Southern Armories often made less-sophisticated copies of Northern designs, like the Spiller & Burr revolver. The fearsome Gatling Gun was also a product of this period. But although it was a devastating weapon, it was rejected by the authorities and never made it into the fight.

The Frontier period followed the Civil War, and firearms continued to develop. Many wartime weapons were still in use, but the gun manufacturers became increasingly ingenious. The first revolvers developed into the double-action type that used centerfire cartridges. These were a far cry from the early percussion cap guns of the pre-war years. Briefly, rifles returned to the single-shot type with the introduction of the excellent Remington Rolling Block and Winchester Low and High wall types. These were designed by John M. Browning and built by famous custom gunsmiths such as George C. Schoyen and Carlos Gove. The military also resorted to the single shot Springfield-Allin trapdoor design in this period. It was as if military commanders were afraid of wasting ammunition. But these guns soon became obsolete when Browning introduced semi-automatic and slide-action repeating designs for both rifles. He also designed updates for the Remington Model 12, the M1911, the Auto-5 and Remington Model 11 shotguns. With the First World War looming Browning went on to develop his military machine gun, culminating in the M2 design and the Browning Automatic Rifle (BAR).

Arming the troops was vital in the time of war, and the Springfield M1903 rifle proved itself in the trenches of France.

Firearms continued to develop in the inter-war years. The prohibition period saw the rise of gang violence and organized crime. Criminals often favored the latest guns, including the Thompson submachine gun.

The outbreak of hostilities after the attack on Pearl Harbor resulted in an unprecedented surge in weapons technology. Newly designed guns like the M1 rifle and carbine and the M3A1 "grease gun" meant that the American fighting man was equipped with weapons equal to those in enemy hands.

After World War II, guns became inextricably linked to popular American culture and became the stuff of books and movies. The Colt Detective Special is a particularly famous model, celebrated in many crime thrillers, while the Smith & Wesson Model 29 needs no introduction to anyone who has seen the Dirty Harry movies. The Calico carbine is equally familiar to fans of Robocop.

In contemporary times, the role of firearms held by civilians has changed substantially. For example, the Mossberg 500 shotgun is primarily sold for home security, as well as having a military role.

The second half of the twentieth century saw America involved in several conflicts, such as Korea and Vietnam, and it was important that American forces continued to have the most up-to-date equipment. In this century's conflicts in the Middle East and Afghanistan, American forces have been armed with guns like the M14, M16 and the Mac-10. These firearms have served the forces well and have maintained America's proud reputation for innovative arms manufacture.

The fifty different firearms featured in this volume represent a chain of firearms innovation that threads its way through America's history.

The American Longrifle

Type: American Longrifle	
Origin: H.E. Leman Conestoga Rifle Works, Lancaster, Pennsylvania	
Caliber: .38	

This weapon grew to prominence in the early to mid 1700s on the American Frontier as it was then, the Appalachian mountain regions of Southeastern Pennsylvania, West Virginia, Tennessee, Kentucky, Ohio, and North Carolina. The gun was known as the Pennsylvania (and later as the Kentucky) Longrifle. It was named for its long-rifled barrel, which was often in excess of 48 inches, but for practical reasons never any higher than the chin of the shooter. You had to see down the end of the barrel to load it properly. This style of gun was very unlike the smooth-bore trade and military muskets of the colonizing powers. It sprang from the experience of immigrant Swiss and German gunsmiths, who used their skills to design weapons that would work well in the "New World." The long-rifled barrel both gave added accuracy and allowed more time for the slow-burning black powder to build up its maximum muzzle velocity. Smaller caliber bullets ranging from .32 to .45 could be used to greater effect and make more economical use of both lead and powder on a protracted hunting expedition or military campaign. In the right hands the gun was effective up to 250 yards. Marksmen like David Crockett and Daniel Boone made it the stuff of legends. Crockett named his gun "ole Betsy" after a favored elder sister. An accredited shot by Boone put a bullet through the forehead of a British officer at a measured distance of 250

Right: An example of the curly maple used for stocking, which was the most popular wood for this type of rifle.

Below: A Pensylvania Longrifle of the Federal Period 1775-1830. The rifle has a 39.5-inch octagonal barrel of .38 caliber and elegant brass American Eagle inlay and patch box on a tiger stripe maple stock.

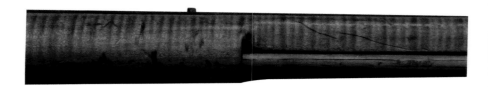

yards, at the 1778 siege of Boonesborough, in Kentucky, when the officer unwisely stuck his head out from behind a tree.

The US military armory at Harpers Ferry began to copy features of the longrifle in their 1792 Contract Rifle.

These guns were often quite ornate, depending somewhat on the affluence of the owner, but fancy carved stocks, silver patch box covers, and engraved locks were much in demand. Curly maple was the favored wood, with elaborately scrolled trigger guards and other stock furniture, reminiscent of the Germanic "Jaeger" style. One of the earliest recorded exponents of the art of Pennsylvania longrifle production is the Swiss-German Mennonite gunsmith Martin Meylin, whose gunshop was established in 1719 in Willow Street, Pennsylvania on the very appropriately named Long Rifle Road.

Above: A plaque commemorating the site of Martin Meylin's gunshop in Willow Street, Pennsylvania.

Other rifle makers sprung up along the Great Wagon Road, a thoroughfare which gave access from the Eastern Seaboard to the interior of the continent and to the South.

Above: A metal can is for gunpowder and bears the picture of an Indian standing with a rifle; it was probably handed over at the same time as the treaty rifles.

Left: The small workshop where Martin Meylin plied his trade still survives 300 year later.

The road wound from Philadelphia, eastern Pennsylvania, through the Shenandoah Valley, into the Cumberland Gap to Kentucky and the Yadkin Valley of North Carolina; it eventually finished in Augusta, Georgia. It was a vital artery, supplying goods and stimulating the growth of the original states.

The design of the gun altered little from its first arrival around 1719 to the 1860s; in this time the ignition system had changed from flintlock to percussion cap. Many guns were converted to percussion and some were changed back again.

Our first featured gun is a plain rifle that appears to have seen much use but which has been treated with care. The simple patch box served its purpose and was easier to open and close than its more elaborate counterparts. The rifled barrel was the most expensive part of any longrifle; the gunsmith spent a lot of time straightening, finishing, and rifling a barrel blank. The original owner probably could not afford the extra time it took to create a 4-piece patch box, elaborate carving, or silver inlays. Later, the owner had the rifle converted to percussion ignition and had the more expensive double set triggers installed. Clearly, the man who owned this rifle was not well-to-do. It is a working man's rifle.

Above: Legendary Frontiersman Davy Crocket with his longrifle, which he nicknamed "Ole Betsy," painted by William Henry Huddle in 1889.

Below: Shown here is a full-stock rifle, with a .45 caliber, 39.25-inch octagonal barrel, walnut stock, and brass furniture.

All the brass mounts are original, including the trigger guard, which has been moved an inch to the rear to accommodate the double set triggers that were added later. The barrel was shortened about 4.5 inches from the muzzle to its present length 38.5 inches. The name "H Bayers" stamped on the barrel near the breech is that of the Allegheny County barrel maker. A forend cap is absent as well as a rear ramrod pipe. A poorly fitted percussion lock, used to replace the original when it was converted in the 1830s, was recently replaced using a flintlock

Above and below: This one is altogether more fancy and carries Leman's name, whereas the others are simply marked "Conestoga Iron Works."

Below: A poster for the 1955 movie celebrating the Kentucky rifle starring Chill Wills.

with the exact dimensions of the original. A piece of wood is missing at the muzzle and at the toe near the butt plate.

We also show two examples by Henry E. Leman, who set up his business in Lancaster, Pennsylvania in 1834 as the Conestoga Rifle Works. His rifles were popular with trappers and explorers. In 1837 he received a government contract to supply 1,000 rifles per year, which was then reviewed annually until 1860, giving him a useful income. He also worked on a government contract from the Department of Indian Affairs to supply guns for the Indian Trade.

The settlers in this frontier territory were extremely proficient with their longrifles; they had to be in order to survive. These skills gave the colonial forces an edge against the British during the American Revolution. Bands of elite marksmen like Morgan's Riflemen struck terror into the British at the revolutionary battles of Saratoga and Cowpens and the War of 1812. The longrifle's nickname, the "Kentucky" rifle, stemmed from a popular song "The Hunters of Kentucky" that chronicled Andrew Jackson's victory at the Battle of New Orleans during that war. It can truly be said that the longrifle helped to throw off colonial oppression and gave the United States the freedom it deserved.

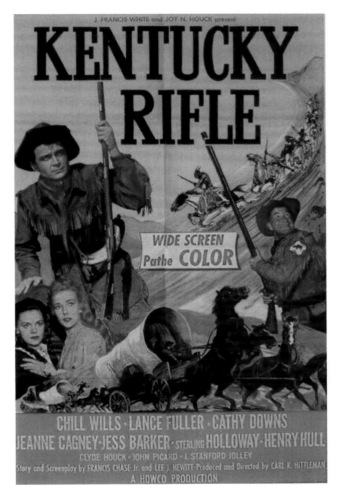

Above: A fine example of a workaday Kentucky Rifle with a massive 48-inch barrel. It is .56 caliber with the traditional carved curly maple stock. The gun has been reconverted to flintlock from Percussion cap using old lock parts. The brass patch box is mostly original.

Browning Automatic Rifle

Type: Light machine gun	
Origin: Various U.S. arsenals	
Caliber: 0.30	
Barrel length: 24 inches	

Opposite page: Clyde Barrow perches on the front fender of his Ford V8, clutching a brace of high powered guns.

John M. Browning first demonstrated his automatic rifle in February 1917. The new weapon weighed just under sixteen pounds. It was perfectly correct to describe it as a rifle, as its general appearance and handling qualities were of this type. The first models had no bipod. In modern terminology, the gun would be described as a squad automatic weapon, as the gun was too light to be a true machine gun and too heavy to be a rifle. Browning did a lot of the initial work on the gas and piston operation of the gun at the Colt factory, but Winchester wase also involved in the later development of the weapon. Manufacture began in 1918, and production totalled 50,000 units. The Allies received the BAR with great enthusiasm, as the weapon was quite unique. They ordered the gun in large quantities, with France ordering 15,000 units. But it was developed too late for extensive service in World War I. The gun was able to fire in bursts or single rounds as required, and later models were equipped with a bipod. Another variation was introduced in 1940, the Model 1918A2, which had a light bipod attached to the tubular flash hider. Although this model fired only in bursts, it also incorporated a selector that allowed two cyclic rates: the higher one was 600; the lower fired 350 rounds per minute. The BAR came to be used in many countries and was also manufactured at Belgium's Herstal factory. A number of the guns were sold to Britain in 1940 and were used to arm the Home Guard, where they gave good service but caused some problems over caliber. The BAR Model 1922 was used by the U.S. Cavalry and had a heavier, finned barrel, a bipod, and a butt rest. It fired automatic rounds only. The gun was also made in special versions for the civilian market and the FBI. The gun was a favored weapon of Clyde Barrow of Bonnie and Clyde fame. Its fearsome firepower kept the federal officers, who were lightly armed with revolvers, at bay.

Left: The Browning BAR was still in active service during the Korean War. Taking cover behind their tank escort, one man of this ranger patrol of the 5th RCT, U.S. 24th Infantry Division, uses his Browning BAR to return the heavy Chinese Communist small arms and mortar fire, which has them pinned down on the bank of the Han River. At left another soldier uses a field radio to report the situation to headquarters.

Browning Semi-Automatic Shotgun

Type: Semi-automatic shotgun

Origin: John Browning/Remington Arms, Co Ilion, New York

Caliber: 12, 16, and 20 gauge

Barrel length: 26 inches

Opposite page: Legendary gun designer John Moses Browning with his auto-loading shotgun. The gun was marketed by Remington in the United States as the Model 11.

One of the most famous shotgun designs of all time, the Browning Auto-5 was not only the very first reliable automatic shotgun, but was also so successful that it remained in full production in the same, basically unaltered, design for 96 years—spanning virtually the entire twentieth century. Indeed, it is still available to special order. This is a truly remarkable record for any invention. Browning filed his first patent application for what he termed a "Recoil Operated Firearm" in May 1899, shortly after his return from two years' missionary work for his church, and it seems virtually certain that, despite his religious commitments, the basic ideas must have been turning over in his mind during that enforced sabbatical away from the drawing board and workshop. While this and later self-loading shotguns are referred to as "automatic," they are actually semi-automatic weapons that need a pull on the trigger to fire each shell.

Browning's new shotgun was covered by four U.S. patents: 659,507/1900 for the basic gun design, 689,283/1901 for the final design, 710,094/1902 covering a number of component improvements, and 812,326/1906 detailing further improvements to the mechanism. To design an automatic shotgun was revolutionary enough, but John Browning carried out this work at a time when smokeless powder was being introduced and manufacturers had not yet solved the problems of variations in load, which could lead to catastrophic events such as split barrels. Indeed, the first automatic shotgun to be sold in the United States was made by a French company named Clair of St Etienne; it was sold from 1895 onwards but was extremely unreliable for this very reason. Such difficulties taxed manually loaded shotgun designers, but they were even more of a problem in an automatic action. Yet John M. Browning solved them all, primarily because of his recent experience in designing and developing automatic pistols and rifles. John Browning's autoloader used the long recoil system, where, on firing, the gasses from the cartridge caused the

Below: An example with a 26-inch solid ribbed barrel.

Opposite page: The Model 11 was hugely popular with hunters. The man on the left has bagged a rabbit and proudly displays his auto-loading shotgun.

barrel and bolt, which at this stage were locked together, to recoil over a distance marginally greater than the length of the shell. At this point the bolt was held back while the barrel was released and driven forwards again by the return spring. The used shell case was retained momentarily by the bolt, and as soon as the chamber had uncovered it, was ejected. The bolt was then released to travel forward, cocking the action and chambering a new shell as it went. The gun was then ready to be fired again.

This is, of course, an oversimplification of a complicated process. The shells were housed in a tubular *magazine* beneath the barrel, which housed five rounds— hence the name "Auto-5." The other name for this shotgun is "Old Humpback," derived from the unique and instantly recognizable shape of the vertical back to the action.

The design was originally offered to Winchester, then to Remington, and, finally, to Fabrique Nationale of Belgium. The latter could not contain its enthusiasm and had the new design in production by 1903, and under the terms of the initial contract, the first batches off the production line were shipped to the Browning brothers in Ogden, Utah, in September of that year. These early batches were in 12-gauge only and were in four grades of finish and four barrel lengths: 26, 28, 30, and 32 inches. The original models were: Standard (also known as Regular), Trap, Messenger, and Two-Shot Automatic. The term "Messenger Gun" was in common usage at the time and denoted a shotgun with a shortened barrel, which was intended for self-defense by people such as guards, couriers, and messengers. The Two-Shot Automatic was produced to meet the needs of people such as the police who considered that the full complement of shells was unnecessary in law enforcement and a smaller number was preferable.

In late 1903 Browning renegotiated his contract with FN and was released from his obligation to import Auto-5s into the United States, while FN continued to hold the license to market the weapon in the whole world, less the United States. Browning then leased the U.S. license to Remington, who started production in 1905, changing its name to the Model 11 in 1911 and going on to manufacture some 850,000 of all types of the Browning design before production ended in 1948.

Calico Light Weapons Systems

Type: Semi-automatic rifle
Origin: Calico, Bakersfield, California
Caliber: .22LR
Barrel length: 17.25 inches

Calico Light Weapons Inc. (CLWS) is a privately held manufacturing company based in Cornelius, Oregon. The company was established in 1982 in Bakersfield, California, and released its first production weapon in 1985. Calico was sold in 1990 but remained in Bakersfield. The company was sold again in 1991 to the original concept designer, and in 1998 operations were moved to Sparks, Nevada, where replacement parts for existing weapons were produced.

In 2006, Calico was sold once again and moved to Hillsboro, Oregon, where full production of firearms resumed. Calico implemented a CNC machining process and upgraded materials used in manufacture. Additionally, there were minor redesigns of some production models to increase durability and reliability.

Below: A Model 100 with a military-style folding butt.

The Calico company produces a series of futuristic-looking semi-automatic weapons, first marketed in 1985. In fact they are relatively straightforward blowback weapons, but the exterior is dominated by the large helical magazine that sits on top of the receiver and holds up to 100 rounds. The Model 100 and Model 100S are both chambered for .22LR and have 17.25-inch barrels, and differ only in that the first has a folding butt and is intended for tactical military use, while the second is for sporting use.

Below: The Model 900 is chambered for 9mm and has a 16-inch barrel.

Above: This Model M950 is classed as a semi-automatic carbine and features a vertical foregrip to steady the gun under fire.

The Calico M950 is as semi-automatic carbine. Its main feature, along with all the other guns of the Calico system, is the feed from the proprietary helical magazine mounted on top, available in 50 or 100-rounds capacity.

The Calico has enough barrel to enable attachment of a vertical foregrip, which is more suited to a submachine gun or a rifle. The factory sights enable reasonable accuracy to about 60 meters (197 feet), but 100 meters is a reasonable range.

Because of the futuristic appearance of the Calico range, it has been used in countless movies and TV shows.

Below: Here the M950A demonstartes its impressive firepower in *RoboCop*.

Colt Model 1860 Army

Type: Percussion revolver
Origin: Colt PFA Mfg. Co., Hartford, Conneticut
Caliber: .44
Barrel length: 7.5 and 8 inches

The production figures for the Colt Model 1860 are self-explanatory—the total produced between 1860 and 1873 was 200,500, of which the U.S. government accepted no less than 127,156. Designed as the successor to the Third Model Dragoon, it became one of the most widely used of all handguns during the Civil War and was equally popular with both the Union and Confederate armies.

The Model Army was a percussion revolver, with rammer loading from the front of the cylinder, and any reasonably experienced shooter ensured that he had a stock of paper cartridges close at hand for rapid reloading. The weapon weighed 2.74 pounds and was fitted with either a 7 1/2, or 8-inch barrel.

Right: Sergeant Stephen Clinton (right) poses with a comrade from the Sixth Virginia Cavalry. Clinton has a large Colt .44-inch Army revolver in his belt, while the second man has a smaller Colt, probably a Model 1849.

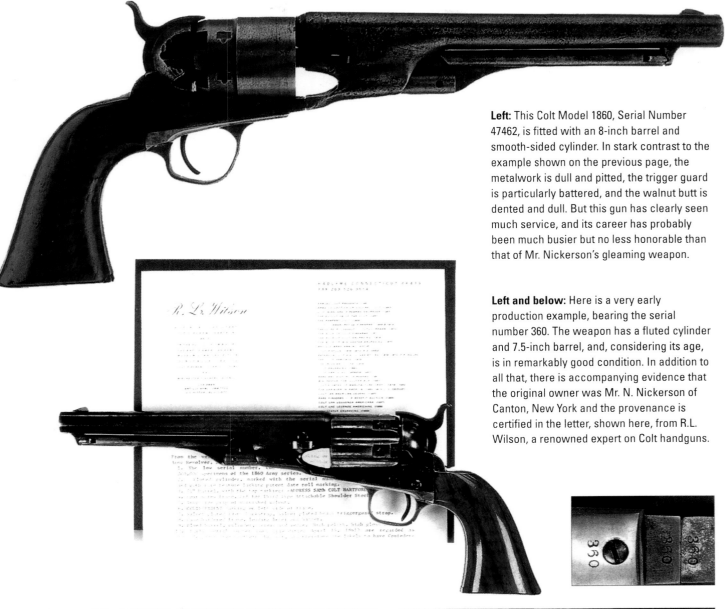

Left: This Colt Model 1860, Serial Number 47462, is fitted with an 8-inch barrel and smooth-sided cylinder. In stark contrast to the example shown on the previous page, the metalwork is dull and pitted, the trigger guard is particularly battered, and the walnut butt is dented and dull. But this gun has clearly seen much service, and its career has probably been much busier but no less honorable than that of Mr. Nickerson's gleaming weapon.

Left and below: Here is a very early production example, bearing the serial number 360. The weapon has a fluted cylinder and 7.5-inch barrel, and, considering its age, is in remarkably good condition. In addition to all that, there is accompanying evidence that the original owner was Mr. N. Nickerson of Canton, New York and the provenance is certified in the letter, shown here, from R.L. Wilson, a renowned expert on Colt handguns.

Colt Model 1911

Type: Semi-automatic pistol

Origin: Colt Patent Fire Arms Mfg.Co., Hartford , CT

Caliber: .45 ACP

Barrel length: 5 inches

Overall length: 8.5 inches

Weight: 2 lbs 7 oz

Right: Doughboys proudly display their new semi-automatic pistols before heading off to Europe to fight in the First World War. Although 100,000 units had been delivered to the US military prior to the War this proved to be nowhere near enough.

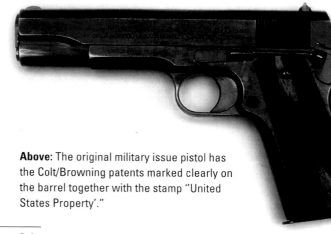

Above: The original military issue pistol has the Colt/Browning patents marked clearly on the barrel together with the stamp "United States Property'."

In the latter part of the nineteeth century, the US handgun scene was dominated by the revolver, and despite the fact that Colt was a major producer, the company was one of the first to recognize that the future lay with the automatic pistol. John M. Browning had already patented several gas-operated self-loading pistols, with Colt buying the rights to each, although the guns never went into production. Browning revised his designs several times and Colt finally put his US patent number 580,924 of 1897 into production as the Colt Model 1900. This gun was chambered for the .38 ACP (Automatic Colt Pistol) cartridge, was 9 inches long, and weighed 2 pounds 3 ounces. However, the real key to success of any weapon at this time was to have it adopted by the US Army.

The army tested many of Colt's designs extensively over a period stretching from 1907 to 1911, finally deciding to buy a modified version of the Model 1905. This gun included general improvements and in some cases fairly radical changes—resultant both from Browning's continuing design "rethinks" and the army's practical requirements passed back from use in the field. This resulted in the Colt Model 1911, which has been described as a design classic which remained in front line army service for well over seven decades. The first delivery of military models was made on January 4, 1912 at a cost to the government of $14.25 for each pistol and one magazine. The gun used the new .45 ACP round, which delivered more than adequate stopping power. The original production weapon was 8.5 inches long with a 3.75-inch (later extended to a 5-inch) barrel and weighed 2 pounds 7 ounces. There were fixed sights on the slide, which had the familiar serrations on either side to enable the shooter to cock it in slippery battlefield conditions. Unlike earlier Models, there were three safety devices: a thumb-operated manual, the grip (John Browning's patent) and a magazine safety. Up to the outbreak of World War I, some 100,000 Model 1911s had been delivered to the US Army, Navy and Marine Corps, but these proved to be nowhere near sufficient. During the final two years of the war, Remington also manufactured the pistol producing 21,676 to Colt's 488,850. During the 1920s, various improvements were made, resulting in the Model 1911 A1 that was approved in 1923. The changes were relatively minor; the hammer spur was extended and there was chamfering behind the trigger. Less visible changes, such as alterations to the lands in the barrel and the magazine retaining mechanism, were also made.

The gun was finally available in three main calibers: the original .45 followed by .38 and .22, all of them in various grades of finish—while a special barrel and magazine were produced in .455 caliber to meet a British World War I order.

Top: A U.S. serviceman crouches, ready for action, with the reassuring weight and power of the Colt in his hand.

Above: The Model that followed, the 1911 A1, incorporated several improvements, including changes to the hammer shape, larger butt safety catch and chamfered cut outs in the frame behind the trigger. This later Variant has a drilled out trigger to save weight.

Left: The pistol was still a strong contender in WWII. This classic poster shows an iconic image of a GI with the gun in hand.

Colt Detective Special

Type: Double-action revolver
Origin: Colt PFA Mfg. Co., Hartford, Connecticut
Caliber: see text
Barrel Length: 2 inches

The Colt Detective Special is a carbon steel framed double-action short-barreled revolver,. It is an example of a class of firearms known to gun enthusiasts as "snubnosed," "snubbies," or "belly guns." As the name "Detective Special" suggests, this model revolver was mainly used as a concealed weapon by plainclothes police detectives.

Introduced in 1927, the Detective Special was one of the first short-barreled revolvers produced with a modern swing-out frame. From the outset, it was

Above: A Colt detective Model in blued finish with .38 Special ammunition.

Right: Humphrey Bogart as Private Detective Philip Marlowe in the film version of Raymond Chandler's *The Big Sleep* packs the trademark Colt Detective.

designed to be chambered for higher-powered cartridges such as the .38 Special, considered to be a powerful caliber for a concealable pocket revolver of the day. The guns were worn in shoulder holsters and other body-mounted devices, including one on on the lower leg.

Above: Gene Hackman as Popeye Doyle in *French Connection II* steadies his aim with his Colt Detective Special.

The Cobra was developed from the Detective Special, but had an alloy frame that reduced its weight from twenty-two ounces to fifteen ounces and was in production from 1950 to 1973. It was available in .22 LR, .32, or .38 Special, and most of those produced had a two-inch barrel. A variant was the "Aircrewman Special," which weighed a mere eleven ounces, but was never sold commercially. Shown here is an excellent example of the Cobra, chambered for .38 Special, and with a two-inch barrel, nickel-plated finish, and walnut grips.

Colt Dragoon

Type: Single-action percussion revolver
Origin: Colt PFA Mfg Co., Hartford, Connecticut
Caliber: .44
Barrel Length: 7.5 inches

Colt Dragoon 1st Model

The earlier Colt Walker revolver (also known as the Whitneyville–Walker or Colt Model 1847) was designed for use by the United States Mounted Rifles (USMR), who were also known by their European name of "Dragoons." The Walker was a six-shot, .44 caliber weapon with a 9-inch barrel and an overall length of 15.5 inches, which weighed no less than four pounds nine ounces. This, plus unreliability problems, led to the development of the Colt Dragoon, or Model 1848, of which some 20,000 were produced for government service

Above: Viewed here from the right side the Colt Dragoon is a formidable looking weapon.

Right: Clint Eastwood as the outlaw Josey Wales in the 1976 movie hefts a pair of Colt Dragoons.

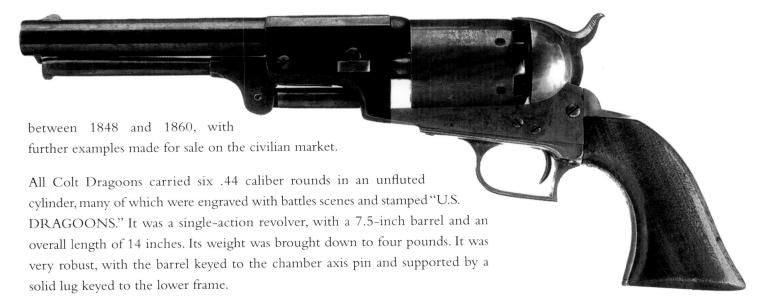

between 1848 and 1860, with further examples made for sale on the civilian market.

All Colt Dragoons carried six .44 caliber rounds in an unfluted cylinder, many of which were engraved with battles scenes and stamped "U.S. DRAGOONS." It was a single-action revolver, with a 7.5-inch barrel and an overall length of 14 inches. Its weight was brought down to four pounds. It was very robust, with the barrel keyed to the chamber axis pin and supported by a solid lug keyed to the lower frame.

The Dragoon was made in three production runs that differed in only minor details, although these differences are of immense importance to today's historians and collectors. The one shown above is the First Model, the main distinguishing feature being that the notches on the cylinder are oval-shaped. Some 7,000 First Model Dragoon revolvers were made in 1848–50, and the item shown here was one of those made for individual purchase rather than for agovernment contract.

Below left: The close-up of the frame and cylinder reveals that the finish on this gun is probably not original.

Below: The detail shows a clear stamping of Colt's Patent and the U.S. government mark.

Type: Single-action percussion revolver

Origin: Colt PFA Mfg Co., Hartford, Connecticut

Caliber: .44

Barrel Length: 8 inches

Colt Dragoon 3rd Model

Building on the success of the Dragoon, Colt introduced a Second Model Dragoon, which differed from the First Model in having rectangular cylinder notches. Some 2,500 were made in 1850 through 1851. The most successful version of the Dragoon, however, was the Third Model, the main production version. Over 10,000 of these were completed in 1851 through 1860, and they can be identified by the round trigger guard, whereas the guards on the earlier two versions were square-backed. The Third Model also had notches for attaching a shoulder stock, although such stocks were seldom, so far as is known, issued. Some late-production Third Model Dragoons (such as the one shown here) had a slightly longer 8-inch barrel.

Above: The 3rd Model has a conventional round trigger guard.

Below: A Colt Dragoon 1848 second model with the squareback trigger guard

Colt Model 1848 Baby Dragoon

Even though Samuel Colt was busy producing weapons for the military, he still managed to find the time to design and produce lighter weapons for the civilian market. One of the first of these was the Model 1848, also known as the "Baby Dragoon," a five-round, .31 caliber weapon, of which some 15,500 were produced in 1848 through 1850. These were made with 3-inch, 4-inch, 5-inch or, as seen here, 6-inch barrels. Many saw wartime service as privately purchased secondary weapons.

Type: Percussion revolver

Origin: Colt PFA Mfg Co., Hartford, Connecticut

Caliber: .31

Barrel Length: 3 inches, 4 inches, 5 inches and 6inches

Above: The Baby Dragoon shared the notched trigger guard with its big brother.

Below: A Baby Dragoon made by Colonel Colt's London factory. Colt's revolvers represented a major export income for the US economy at this time.

Above: John Wayne as Rooster Cogburn
steadies a Colt Dragoon on the shoulder of
Kim Darby as Mattie Ross in *True Grit*.

Colt Model 1878 Frontier

The Colt Model 1878 appeared shortly after the Model 1877 and was another double-action revolver. But it was larger and more robust, with a strong frame and a removable trigger guard. The fluted cylinder held six cartridges and was not removable, being loaded via a narrow gate on the right side of the frame. There were six barrel lengths (3, 3.5, 4, 4.75, 5.5, and 7.5 inches) and a wide variety of chambering from .22 to .476. The gun is instantly recognizable by the disc on the side of the frame behind the cylinder. It was popular with a number of Western characters, including Pawnee Bill

Type: Colt Model 1878 Frontier
Caliber: 0.44-.40
Length of barrel: 4 inches
Barrel shape: Round

Lilly, who taught his wife May to become a crack shot using a Frontier. Rose Dunn, "The Rose of Cimarron," and a member of the Doolin Gang also favored the gun. A total of some 51,000 were produced in 1878 through 1905, which included

Above and left: The Frontier was widely used in the American West. This example, one of a series known as the Sheriff's Model, was used by Sheriff J.H. Ward of Vinta County, as shown by the engraving on the backstrap. His revolver was .44-40 caliber and had a 4.5-inch barrel.

Right: Rose Dunn, a.k.a The Rose of Cimarron, is pictured with her Colt Model 1878 in .45 caliber.

Below: Rose with her Colt in the 1952 movie based on her life.

4,000 Model 1878/1902, ordered by the U.S. Army in 1902 for use in Alaska and the Philippines.

This example, one of a series known as the "Sheriff's Model," was used by Sheriff J.H. Ward of Vinta County, as shown by the engraving on the backstrap. His revolver was .44–.40 caliber and had a 4.5-inch barrel.

Ward was sheriff from 1886 to 1912 and was responsible for capturing and bringing in Butch Cassidy. Significantly, he was also a party to Cassidy's parole.

Colt Model 1878 Alaskan Model

In 1902, 4,600 Model 1878 revolvers were produced for a U.S. Army contract. They were intended to equip the Philippine Constabulary under Brigadier General Henry T. Allen in the Philippine Insurrection. These revolvers had a 6-inch barrel, a hard rubber grip, and were chambered for the .45 Colt round. They had a strengthened main spring and a longer trigger to give the user more leverage, resulting a larger trigger guard. The strengthened main spring was necessary to fire the .45 Government rounds with a less sensitive primer compared to the civil .45 LC ammunition. Many people have incorrectly assumed that this was to allow the revolver to be operated while wearing gloves, so "Alaskan Model" is a misnomer.

Type: Center–fire double-action revolver	
Origin: Colt PFA Mfg. Co., Hartford, Connecticut	
Caliber: .45 Colt	
Barrel length: 6 inches	

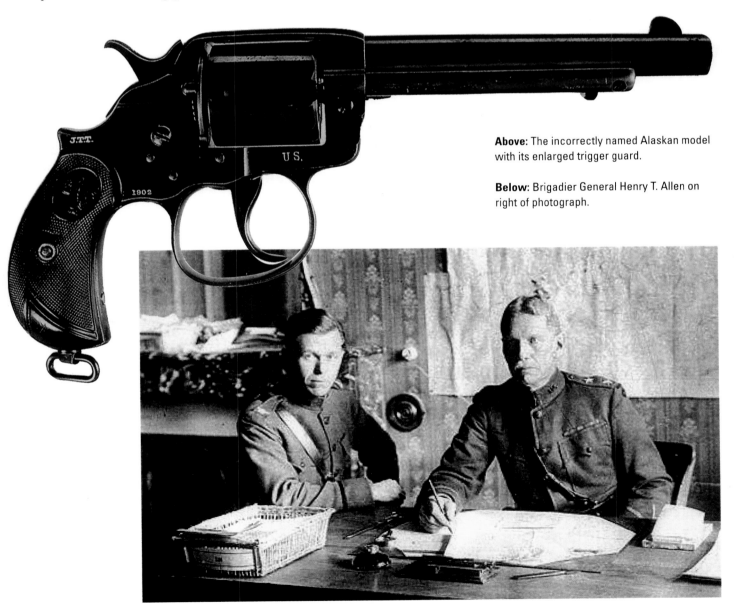

Above: The incorrectly named Alaskan model with its enlarged trigger guard.

Below: Brigadier General Henry T. Allen on right of photograph.

Colt Lightning

Type: Center-fire, double-action revolver

Origin: Colt PFA Mfg Co., Hartford, Connecticut

Caliber: Lightning .38 Colt; Thunderer .41 Colt

Barrel Length: see text

Below John Wesley Hardin on his wedding day in 1877. Like many outlaws, his involvement with powerful handguns brought about his early demise.

Samuel Colt was not keen on the idea of double-action revolvers, but when effective systems appeared from other manufacturers the company had little choice but to follow suit. The first Colt double-action revolver was the Model 1877 which appeared in two forms, .38 caliber, known as the Lightning, and .41 caliber, known as the Thunderer; both were six-shooters, and both came in a variety of barrel lengths.

In appearance, the Model 1877 resembled a slightly scaled down Single-Action Army, except for the butt that was a bird's head shape made of hard rubber or wood. Both types proved over-complicated and were very difficult to repair; even so, some 166,000 were made between 1877 and 1909. The Lightning was chambered for the .38 Colt and came in three barrel lengths. All are shown here: 4.5-inch (complete with ejector rod); 3.5-inch, and 2.5-inch (note the cylinder arbor with a knurled head, which had to be unscrewed and the cylinder removed completely before the cartridge cases could be removed).

As handguns grew more sophisticated and had a higher rate of fire, they were sought out by not only lawmen but criminals. One such was John Wesley Hardin, who claimed to have killed at least forty men. Hardin moved to El Paso in 1895, where he became a lawyer and settled down to write his autobiography. But Hardin couldn't leave his violent past behind and soon became involved in a cocktail of gambling and gun crime. As a result he was shot down in El Paso's Acme Saloon at the age of forty-two. When he died, Hardin was carrying a .38 caliber, 2.5-inch barreled Colt Model 1877 Lightning revolver with mother-of-pearl grips (serial number 84304). The gun had been presented to him by a grateful client and was shipped to him from the Colt factory in 1891. Unfortunately for him, Wes Hardin never got a chance to draw this elegant firearm from its tooled leather holster that he had bought in El Paso. His previous gun had also been a Colt revolver, an 1877 .41 caliber Thunderer. Hardin had used this gun to hold up and rob the Gem Saloon.

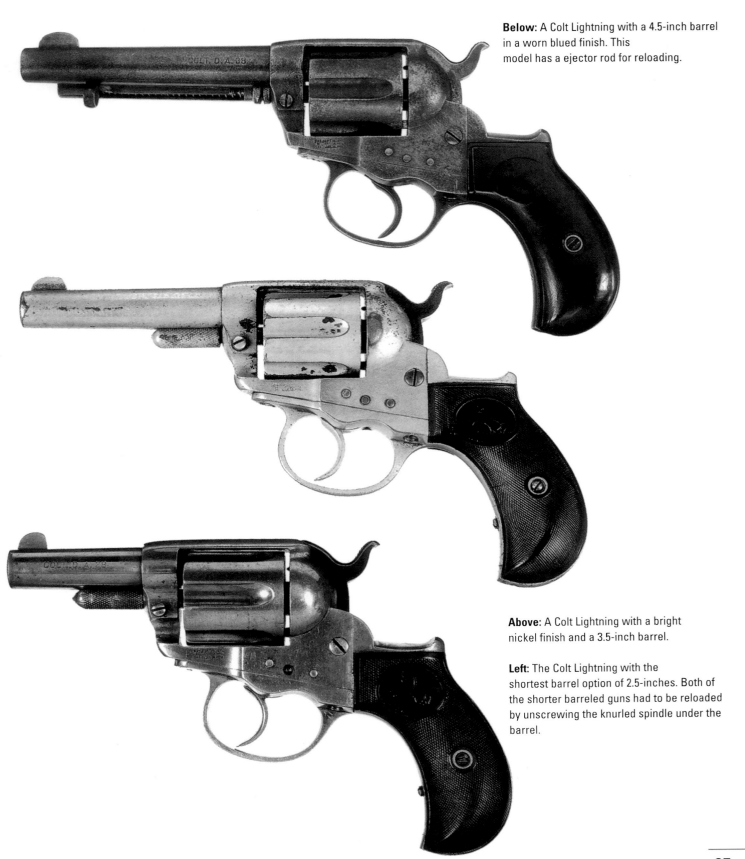

Below: A Colt Lightning with a 4.5-inch barrel in a worn blued finish. This model has a ejector rod for reloading.

Above: A Colt Lightning with a bright nickel finish and a 3.5-inch barrel.

Left: The Colt Lightning with the shortest barrel option of 2.5-inches. Both of the shorter barreled guns had to be reloaded by unscrewing the knurled spindle under the barrel.

Colt M16 Assault Rifle

Type: Assault rifle

Origin: Colt Armaments Mfg. Co., Hartford, Conneticut

Caliber: 5.56mm

Barrel length: 20 inches

In the early 1950s, the Fairchild Aircraft Corporation formed the new "Armalite" division, headed by Eugene Stoner, to pursue recent advances in aluminium alloy and glass-reinforced plastic (GRP) technology. One of the division's first tasks was to look at small arms design, and Stoner, who was an aviation rather than a weapons engineer, started with a clean sheet. After some failed attempts at military caliber rifles, Stoner designed a new rifle (the AR-15) around the lighter .223 cartridge, which was intended for use against the shorter range targets now specified by the U.S. Army. Making extensive use of light alloys and glass-reinforced plastics, the rifle was light, handy, and had minimum recoil. The ammunition was also lighter, and an infantryman caould carry 280 rounds of .223 compared to a hundred rounds of .30. But the army resisted these new concepts, and in February 1959 Fairchild gave up and sold its design rights to Colt.

At much the same time, the commander-in-chief of the U.S. Air Force, General Curtis Le May, chanced to see a live-firing demonsration of the AR-15, which resulted in small numbers being taken into USAF service under the designation, soon to become famous, of M16. The lack of army interest continued until the first combat troops to be deployed to Vietnam noticed the rifle being used by USAF airfield guards, who demanded that they may be issued with them, particularly for jungle fighting.

After many trials and tribulation, the rifle was standardized for all four U.S. forces as the M16, and Colt was soon producing 40,000 per month, with some

Below: The M16 was eventually issued to all troops in Vietnam.

400,000 fielded in South Vietnam by early 1966. Most unfortunately, however, three associated decisions, all taken for reasons of "economy," brought the AR-15/M16 to the verge of disaster. These were: first, that there was no requirement to issue cleaning kits; secondly, that there was no need to crome-plate the chamber; and thirdly, that cheaper "ball" powder should be used in the ammunition.

Reports soon reached Washington from the all-important Vietnam theater that while the M16 had been greeted with enthusiasum, the majority of troops had quickly become seriously disenchanted due to the unreliability of the weapon, which was suffering from

Above: U.S. Marine Corps in action in Vietnam engaged in operation Allen Brook.

Above and left: This is an early production Colt M16, chambered for the .223 M193 round and with a 21-inch barrel and 20-round magazine. The M16 has, of course, been modified and adapted over the years, the original 20-round magazine was replaced by a 30-round version, and various add-ons, such as the M203 grenade-launcher, were devised.

Above: The M16A2 introduced a new heavier barrel with revised rifling enabling it to take the new NATO SS109 5.46mm round. The fully automatic capability was also changed to a three-round burst setting.

Above: The M16A4 is the fourth generation of the M16 series. It is equipped with a removable carrying handle and a full length quad for mounting optics and other ancillary devices. The FN M16A4, using safe/semi/burst selective fire, is now the standard issue for all U.S. Marine Corps.

seemingly endless stoppages. Some of the causes were only too apparent. The official policy of not issuing cleaning kits had led the soldiers to believe that the M16 did not need to be cleaned, a problem that was exacerbated by the failure to chrome the chamber and the use of cheaper powder, all of which combined to produce excessive fouling and hence stoppages. Never has there been a better example of "false economy." Cleaning kits were issued, the chamber chromed and the powder changed, and these, coupled with a return to proper attention to keeping the rifle clean, soon cut the stoppages down to a more acceptable level. Not so immediately obvious, however, was a problem with the bolt, which tended to rebound from the breech-face. Once identified these problems were all solved, and the M16 changed from a disaster into a triumph. It became every infantryman's weapon of choice.

The M16 has been sold to many foriegn armies, to both U.S. and foreign police forces, and also to civilians. It has also been manufactured under license in Canada, South Korea, the Philippines, Singapore, and Taiwan, and a few "sporters" are also known to have been produced by Norinco in China. In addition, the Department of Defense was reluctant to depend upon Colt as the single-source supplier, and in 1968 contracts were placed with General Motors (Hydramatic Division) and Harrington & Richardson.

M16 Sport Variants

Above: Colt has sold a large number of "sporter" models on the civilian market. This one is the AR-15A2 Sporter II (Model 711), based on the original M16, with a 21-inch barrel chambered for the .223 round, and normally sold with a five-round magazine (missing in this picture).

Above: The Sporter Match HBAR (Heavy BARrel) has a 20-inch barrel and TASCO 20x telescopic sight, which is fitted with an extended sunshade.

Below: A Spoter Target Model, with numerous additions for serious target use, including a raised cheek-piece, pistol grip rest, and TASCO 3 x 9 telescopic sight, which is protected by a special rubber coating.

Colt Navy Model 1851

Type: Percussion revolver

Origin: Colt PFA Mfg Co.,
Hartford, Connecticut

Caliber: .36

Barrel Length: 7.5 inches

The Colt Model 1851 Navy revolver was one of the most popular handguns ever made, with some 215,000 manufactured in various Colt factories in 1850 through 1873. It has a 7.5-inch octagonal barrel and a smooth sided cylinder which houses six .36 caliber rounds. In most cases, the cylinder was decorated with a scene involving a naval battle between United States and Mexican fleets. It was this decoration that gave the type its "Navy" designation,

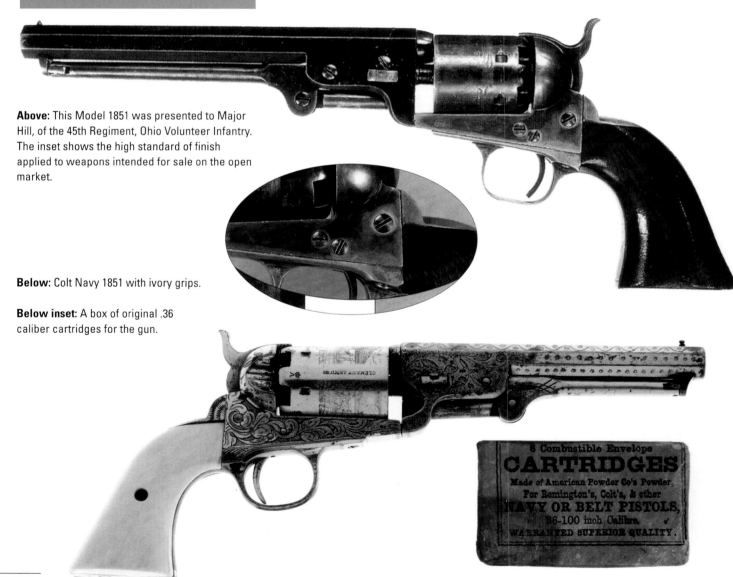

Above: This Model 1851 was presented to Major Hill, of the 45th Regiment, Ohio Volunteer Infantry. The inset shows the high standard of finish applied to weapons intended for sale on the open market.

Below: Colt Navy 1851 with ivory grips.

Below inset: A box of original .36 caliber cartridges for the gun.

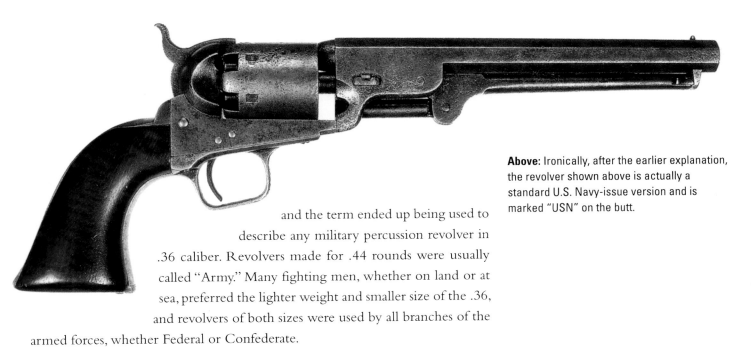

Above: Ironically, after the earlier explanation, the revolver shown above is actually a standard U.S. Navy-issue version and is marked "USN" on the butt.

and the term ended up being used to describe any military percussion revolver in .36 caliber. Revolvers made for .44 rounds were usually called "Army." Many fighting men, whether on land or at sea, preferred the lighter weight and smaller size of the .36, and revolvers of both sizes were used by all branches of the armed forces, whether Federal or Confederate.

A shoulder stock was available for the Model 1851, which could be attached to the butt for more accurate long-range shooting. The company applied three different forms of address on these revolvers, some being marked "Saml. Colt New York City" while others bore "Saml. Colt Hartford, Ct;" there was a yet further variation of "Saml. Colt New York U.S. America."

Below left: An unidentified confederate soldier with a Colt Navy revolver and D-guard bowie knife.

Below: A Civil War era powder flask and bullet mold for the Colt.

Colt Single-Action

Type: Center-fire, single-action revolver
Origin: Colt PFA Mfg. Co., Hartford, Connecticut
Caliber: .45 Colt and .44/40 Winchester
Barrel Length: various, see text

The Colt Single-Action Army revolver or Colt .45 is one of the greatest handguns in history and was not only purchased in vast numbers for the U.S. Army, but was also widely sold on the civilian market, particularly in the American West where it came to symbolize the cowboy era. The civilian model was marketed as the Frontier and was designed to use the same .44/40 ammunition as the Winchester 1873, sharing the title, "the Gun that won the West." This had the advantage that only one type of ammunition needed to be carried to suit a Westerner's handgun and his rifle. The gun's story began in 1872 when the U.S. Army conducted a rigorous competition for a new revolver; this was won by Colt, whose entry was accepted for service as the Model 1873. It was then continuously in production for sixty-seven years (1873-1940) during which time exactly 357,859 were produced. It was reintroduced into production in 1956, and even today the Single-Action Army

Above: The basic Model 1873 was produced in three barrel lengths. This revolver is an early (Serial Number 19393) .45 caliber weapon with a 7.5-inch barrel, showing the elegance of line, with bare metal finish and plain walnut grips.

Above: Another .45 caliber, this one has a 5.5-inch barrel and there is documentary proof that it was carried by Mark Bently of Company M, 6th Massachusetts Volunteer Infantry during the Spanish-American War.

Opposite page: TV hero Clayton Moore as the Lone Ranger draws his Colt .45. His .45 bullets were made of silver as can be seen on his ammunition belt. The Colt 45 was the standard gun in TV westerns of the 1950s.

Above: This one above (.45 caliber 7.5-inch barrel) was made for the civilian market and has a much higher standard of finish; it was shipped to a New York gun dealer on November 1, 1876.

Right: As the poster announces, the single-action was relaunched in 1956 after 15 years of unavailability.

is still available from Colt, although made in very small numbers and at considerable expense.

The gun was the archetypal cowboy's gun and appeared in most Hollywood depictions of the West. Popular with lawmen and outlaws alike, the gun became known as the Peacemaker.

There is nothing particularly unusual about the design and construction of the Model 1873, but the inspired combination of simplicity, ruggedness, ease of use, and dependability has made for an enduring and unpretentious classic.

ONCE AGAIN — THE AUTHENTIC

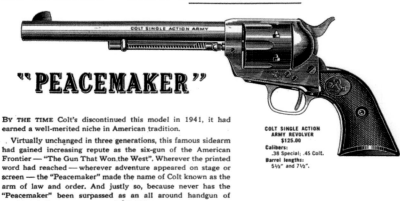

"PEACEMAKER"

COLT SINGLE ACTION ARMY REVOLVER
$125.00
Calibers:
.38 Special; .45 Colt.
Barrel lengths:
5½" and 7½".

BY THE TIME Colt's discontinued this model in 1941, it had earned a well-merited niche in American tradition.

. Virtually unchanged in three generations, this famous sidearm had gained increasing repute as the six-gun of the American Frontier — "The Gun That Won the West". Wherever the printed word had reached — wherever adventure appeared on stage or screen — the "Peacemaker" made the name of Colt known as the arm of law and order. And justly so, because never has the "Peacemaker" been surpassed as an all around handgun of precision, balance, accuracy, and reliability.

Gun enthusiasts the country over have never ceased to clamor for the return of this most famous of all American guns. Because of this, Colt's will re-issue the Colt Single Action Army Revolver this fall, essentially the same as it was originally made in 1873. It will be an item for connoisseurs, as well as hunters, target shooters, and plinkers who love fine weapons. Production will be limited. Place your order now, wherever fine guns are sold.

COLT

COLT'S PATENT FIRE ARMS MANUFACTURING COMPANY
Hartford 15, Connecticut, U.S.A.

There are innumerable examples of strange conversions, elaborately engraved finishes, and weapons with unusual histories, but this one, below, deserves inclusion for its curiosity value. It is a .44 Special Caliber with a 4.75-inch barrel, and was one of fifty shipped to a New York dealer on September 14, 1882. Many years later this revolver, plus the accompanying holster shown here, was used by the legendary Arvo Ojala to teach shooting and fast draws to movie stars such as Clint Eastwood and Sammy Davis Junior. Indeed, the revolver almost certainly appeared in movies as its finish has been improved and the grips revarnished to ensure that it looked good on camera.

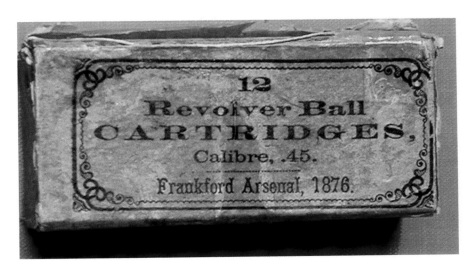

Above and left: An original cartridge box from the Frankford arsenal and different types of .45 ammunition.

The Derringer

Type: see text	
Origin: see text	
Caliber: see text	
Barrel length: see text	

The Derringer was a popular choice as a defensive weapon for frontier women, saloon girls and respectable ladies alike. It was easily concealed in a purse, the pocket of a crinoline dress, or even a garter. It was named for Henry Deringer, a Philadelphia gunsmith who developed a range of compact, high-caliber pocket pistols that, despite their size, had reasonable stopping power. His guns were so successful that his name became synonymous with

Above: A silver plated National Arms Co.1st Model Derringer in .41 caliber.

Right: The Derringer was a favorite with gamblers like these four. Guns were often concealed in vest pockets and became known as "vest" guns.

all weapons of the type. The press report on John Wilkes Booth assassination of Abraham Lincoln wrongly spelled the name of the weapon used as "Derringer" and this version of the name became common usage.

In the early days, many of these guns were single-shot weapons that relied on a well placed first (and only) shot to stave off an attack—the pressure was on to provide better odds. But later developments like the double-shot Derringers gave the shooter two chances instead of one.

During the Wild West period a new breed of men grew up. Clad in tailored jackets and dust-free Derby hats, the gamblers had hit town. Unlike the cowboys, these men did not wear large Colts holstered in plain view, preferring to hide the small, but deadly, Derringers about their person. They were often concealed in a vest pocket, inside a hatband, or in a well-tailored sleeve. The Derringer settled many an accusation of cheating at cards. Over the page is a selection of these weapons of concealment.

Below: A contemporary post card showing the assassination of President Lincoln, which was carried out using a Derringer.

THE ASSASSINATION OF PRESIDENT LINCOLN,
AT FORD'S THEATRE WASHINGTON. D.C. APRIL 14TH 1865.

1 Tipping & Lawden Four-barrel pistol
Four barrels are better than one. Master gunsmiths Tipping & Lawden of Birmingham, England manufactured this Sharps design. It was then imported into the United States. The gun has 3-inch barrels and is .31 caliber. It is lavishly decorated with much engraving and pearl grips.

2, 3, 4 Colt Deringers
These are three examples of the Colt Third Model Deringer. The gun was designed by Alexander Thuer, and was often known as the "Thuer Derringer." All three examples are .41 caliber weapons with 2.5-inch barrels. The barrels pivoted to one side for loading.

5 Hammond Bulldog
This is a crudely finished single-shot self-defense weapon of .44 caliber. Nevertheless, it would be effective at close range. It has a 4-inch barrel and must have kicked like a mule!

6 Hopkins & Allen Vest Pocket Deringer
This cleverly camouflaged trinket was just 1¾ inches long, and fired a .22 caliber round. It could (literally) fit in the palm of the shooter's hand, and be concealed until the last moment.

7 National No. 2 Deringer
Moore's Patent Firearm Company was established in Brooklyn in the mid-nineteenth century. The company changed its name to The National Arms Company in 1866. This gun is the No. 2 Model. It has a spur trigger, and is loaded by dropping the barrel down to one side. Following the takeover of the company by Colt in 1870, this design was marketed as the Colt No. 2 Deringer.

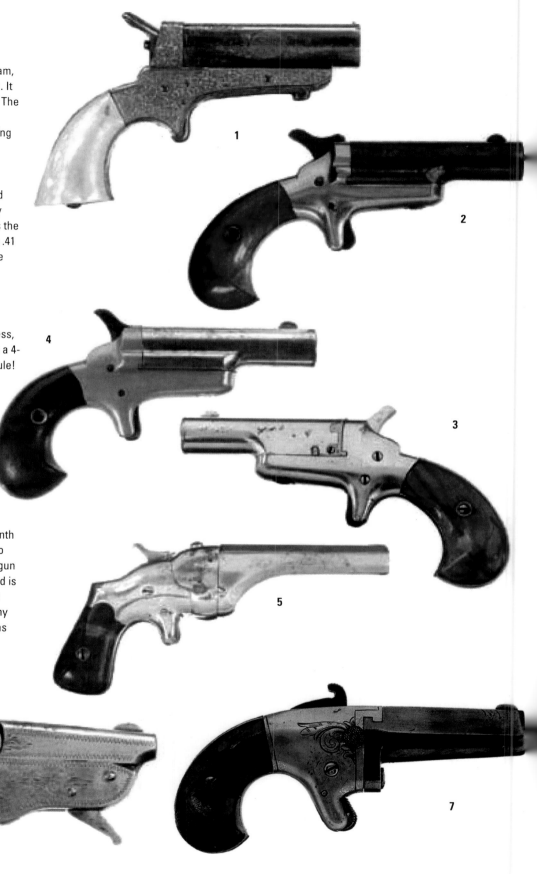

8 Remington Elliot Ring Trigger Pistol
This pistol relied on four solid static barrels to deliver four shots. It was chambered for .32 caliber ammunition. The ring trigger was pushed forward to rotate the firing pin, then pulled back to cock the mechanism and fire.

9 Remington No2 Vest Pocket Pistol
Designed by Joseph Rider, this .32 caliber vest pocket pistol fired a single shot. It was equipped with the unique Rider split-breech loading system, and had a 3¼-inch barrel.

10 Remington Double Deringer
This was the ultimate design for last ditch defense. The over-and-under barrel layout was less cumbersome and heavy than that of multi-barrel guns. The gun was also reliable, and fired two rounds in .41 caliber: an assailant-stopping load. The gun became extremely popular and over 150,000 were manufactured between 1866 and 1935.

11 Sharps Pepperbox
Strictly speaking, this design by master gunsmith Christian Sharps is a multi-barreled pistol rather than a pepperbox. Nonetheless, the gun became a very popular weapon. The gun was reloaded by sliding the barrel block forward along a rail to access the breech. The four-barrel system was static and the firing pin rotated to fire each chamber in turn.

12 Wheeler Double Derringer
This weapon was designed and manufactured by the American Arms Company. It features two vertically mounted barrels that were rotated manually. This example has a 3-inch barrel block, chambered for two .32 caliber rounds. It has a nickel-plated frame, a spur trigger, and blued barrels.

The Gatling Gun

Type: Machine gun

Origin: Colt Armory, Hartford, Connecticut.

Caliber: .45

Barrel length: 10 inches

Doctor Richard J. Gatling invented the first working version of the machine gun in 1862, the second year of the Civil War. The war had stimulated a great deal of weapon development, and Gatling believed that a high rate of automatic gunfire would reduce the number of soldiers needed to man the battlefield, thus reducing their exposure to disease and the hazards

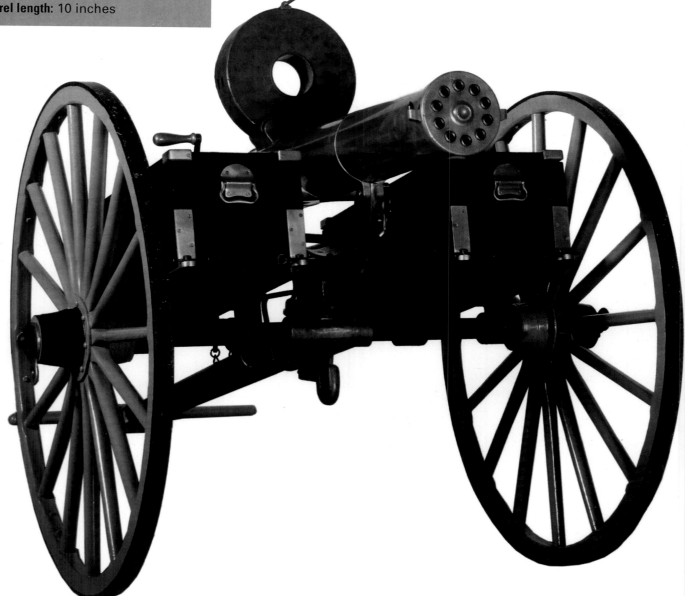

Left: The Gatling gun was used in the Philippines war.

Below: The inventor with a tripod mounted version of the gun.

of war. Gatling demonstrated his first weapon in 1862 in Indianapolis, Indiana, at the age of 44 and patented the gun in the November of that year. The key elements of the gun were a lock cylinder containing six strikers that revolved with six rotating gun barrels, all powered by a hand crank. (Hence Abraham Lincoln's nickname for the Gatling, the "Coffee-Mill gun.") In this sense, the weapon was not yet a true machine gun, as an external power source was required. Gatlings were fed ammunition by means of hoppers, which loaded powder and ball into the steel chambers. This resulted in gas leakage (a fairly common difficulty in revolving arms). Self-contained rim-fire cartridges were then introduced. For the time, the gun attained an extremely high rate of fire of 200 shots per minute. The Colt Armory in Hartford, Connecticut manufactured the production model of the gun. Gatling offered the gun to the Government, and was subsequently turned down by the rather reactionary General Ripley, the Chief of Ordnance. A lighter version of the gun was then introduced, which weighed 135 pounds, which was mounted on a robust wooden tripod, rather like a light cannon.

Hall Breech-loading Rifles

Type: Breech-loading flintlock/ percussion rifle

Origin: Harpers Ferry Armory, Harpers Ferry, Virginia

Caliber: .52

Barrel length: 36.6 inches

Below: A Hall rifle with the breech open.

Bottom: A percussion cap version of the rifle with a cleaning rod.

John Hancock Hall was born in 1781 in Portland, Maine. In his early career he spent time in the militia where he acquired an interest in firearms, particularly the speed of loading which Hall identified as an area ripe for improvement.

Hall worked with a Washington D.C. architect, Dr. William Thornton, to design a novel single shot flintlock breech-loading rifle, which was patented on May 21, 1811. The weapon featured a tip-up breech chamber in which the breech lock and chamber were combined in a single machine part. This was exceedingly advanced for the time. Production of the new rifle was begun in Portland, Maine at a leisurely rate of fifty per year from 1811 to 1816.

During that time the gun had come to the attention of the United States ordnance department, which attempted to order 200 rifles in December 1814. Hall declined the order because his production limitations in Portland meant that he could not possibly meet the Army's delivery deadline of 1815.

In order to overcome his production limitations, Hall reasoned that what slowed down production was rifles being made in the traditional way, with skilled artisans individually hand-crafting components to fit each rifle. By standardizing patterns and components and relying on machinery to make them, Hall introduced a system of "interchangeable parts" that fitted all examples of a Model. His proposal of this concept to the army led to a contract for 1,000 Model 1819 rifles in 1816. Part of the condition of the contract was that Hall relocate to the government armory at Harpers Ferry, Virginia to oversee production of his rifles. He was allocated an old sawmill on Virginius Island in the Shenandoah River as his factory, which soon became known as "Hall's Rifle Works" on "Lower Hall Island."

Left: The ruins of Hall's rifle Works. The stone built sluices controlled the flow of water to millwheels, which supplied the power to the machinery within.

Hall also used the resources of water power by adapting the sawmill's existing millpower technology to turn his lathes and milling machines. A system of leather belts and pulleys transferred the power of the mill wheels to his machinery, giving up to 3,000 revolutions per minute. He designed and built drop hammers, lathes, milling machines, drilling machines, straight, lever, and curved cutting machines. Even his wooden stocks were machine made. This revolutionized production as a relatively unskilled hand could run these machines and, it was reckoned, could produce more work output than ten skilled craftsmen with hand cutters and files.

On December 20, 1822, Hall wrote this rather wordy mission statement to Secretary of War John Calhoun:

"I have succeeded in an object which has hitherto completely baffled (notwithstanding the impressions to the contrary which have prevailed) all the

Below: A Hall rifle with the original flintlock action.

endeavours of those who have heretofore attempted it—I have succeeded in establishing methods for fabricating arms exactly alike, and with economy, by the hands of common workmen, and in such manner as to ensure a perfect observance of any established model, and to furnish in the arms themselves a complete test of their conformity to it."

Hall spent the next few years (and $150,000 of government money) delivering Model 1819s. His success was verified by Colonel George Talcott of the Ordnance Department who wrote in 1832 that Hall's rifles had been manufactured "to a greater degree of perfection, as regards the quality of work and uniformity of parts than is to be found anywhere—almost everything is performed by machinery, leaving very little dependent on manual labor."

The Model 1819 was tested against contemporary muzzle-loading rifles and smooth-bore muskets. A company of marksmen were allowed ten minutes to load and fire each of the three types of weapon.

Using a conventional muzzle-loading rifle the men were able to fire 464 shots in the time allotted and achieved a 33% hit rate. Using a smooth-bore musket which was less accurate but easier to load, they got off 845 shots with a hit rate of 25%. The result for the breech-loading Hall was 1198 shots and a hit rate of 36%. Therefore in ten minutes the marksmen using the Hall Rifles hit 430 targets as opposed to only 164 for the conventional muzzle-loading rifle. This really made the case for breech-loading weapons on the battlefield.

The model ran until it was replaced with the Model 1841, which had the later type percussion ignition. Despite the gun's success due to its improved rate of fire over conventional weapons, at the time it suffered from low power because loss of gas from the movable breech reduced the gun's muzzle velocity. No serious attempts were made to improve the seal between the breech and the barrel other than to prescribe a heavier charge to compensate. Although the model broke ground in 1811, it was already lagging behind in 1841 when Hall died.

The changes that John Hancock Hall really

Below: The Hall stamp on a breech mechanism.

brought about were more to do with his production techniques. Men who worked for him at Harpers Ferry went on to apply those methods to manufacture shoes, watches, clocks, bicycles, clothing, and later, automobiles. His attention to uniformity and interchangeable manufacture laid the foundation for the later development of America's successful factory system.

Above: The interior of a typical nineteenth-century machine workshop. The machines were driven by the leather belts from the overhead shaft, which in turn connected to the shaft from the millwheels taking power from the stream below.

Harpers Ferry Model 1841 Mississippi Rifle

Type: Muzzle-loading, percussion rifle

Origin: Harpers Ferry Armory, Harpers Ferry, Virginia

Caliber: .54

Barrel Length: 33 inches

Above: Harpers Ferry is situated at the confluence of the Potomac and the Shenandoah rivers.

Right: The armory at Harpers Ferry was set afire during John Brown's raid in 1859.

The town of Harpers Ferry is situated at the confluence of the Potomac and Shenandoah rivers where the U.S. states of Maryland, Virginia and West Virginia meet. The ferry originally provided access across the river to enable Westward expansion.

In 1796 the federal government purchased a 125-acre parcel of land from the heirs of original landowner Robert Harper to construct the United States Armory and Arsenal at Harpers Ferry. This was one of only two such facilities in the U.S., the other being at Springfield, Massachusetts. Together they produced most of the small arms for the U.S. Army.

When production of the Hall breechloading rifle ended in 1841, the Harpers Ferry "rifle works" was converted to manufacture the newly adopted U.S. Model 1841 rifle. Some 25,000 were produced at Harpers Ferry between 1846 and 1855. The Model 1841 will always be known as the "Mississippi rifle" in memory of the troops who used it during the Mexican-American War, particularly at the Battle of Buena Vista against General Santa Anna's Mexican army in February 1847. In that battle, Colonel Jefferson Davis's 1st Mississippi Rifles, armed with the new muzzle-loading "U.S. Model 1841 Percussion Rifle," turned the tide for the heavily outnumbered U.S. troops,

and this weapon has been known ever since been known as the Mississippi rifle in their honor.

The town was transformed into an industrial center; between 1801 and 1861, when an attempt was made to destroy it to prevent capture. During the Civil War, the armory produced more than 600,000 muskets, rifles, and pistols. Due to its location the town changed hands several times during the War and at the cessation of hostilities was never used as an arsenal again.

Below: This example is dated 1850 and appears to be in original condition and is complete except for the sling swivels.

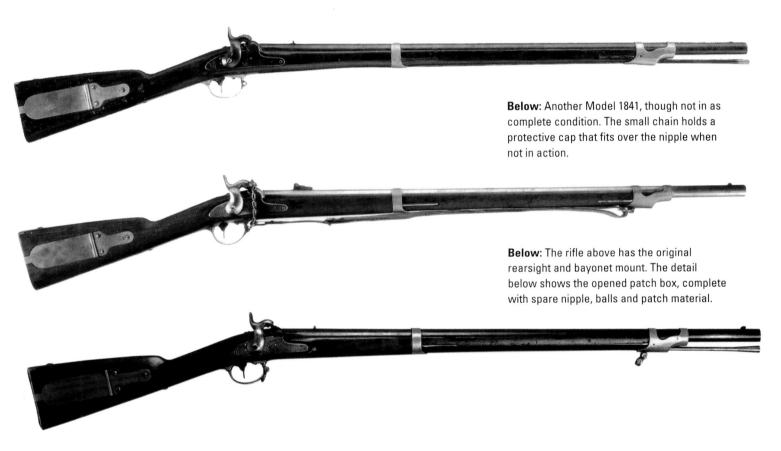

Below: Another Model 1841, though not in as complete condition. The small chain holds a protective cap that fits over the nipple when not in action.

Below: The rifle above has the original rearsight and bayonet mount. The detail below shows the opened patch box, complete with spare nipple, balls and patch material.

Left: Discovered in a Model 1841 patch box are the remnants of battle: some musket balls, wadding and spare percussion nipple.

Published by R. Magee

CAPT BRAGG'S ARTILLERY AT THE B

"GIVE 'EM A LITTLE MORE GRAPE CAP

TLE OF BUENA VISTA

No, 45 Chisnut St. near 2d Phil.

Left: Jefferson Davis and his men scored a decisive victory over the Mexicans at the Battle of Buena Vista using Model 1841's.

Henry Rifle

Type: Tubular-magazine lever-action rifle

Origin: New Haven Arms,Co., New Haven, Connecticut

Caliber: .44 Henry

Barrel length: 24.25 inches

The origins of this groundbreaking rifle lie in the ashes of the Volcanic Repeating Arms Company, which specialized in repeating lever action pistols. In 1857 after an unsuccessful run of just 3,000 pistols, the company was declared bankrupt and Oliver Winchester, who was already serving as vice president and who was a major investor, took over and formed the New Haven Arms Company.

Right: A poster makes some dramatic claims for the Henry rifle.

Below: Plant superintendent B Tyler Henry gave his name to the gun.

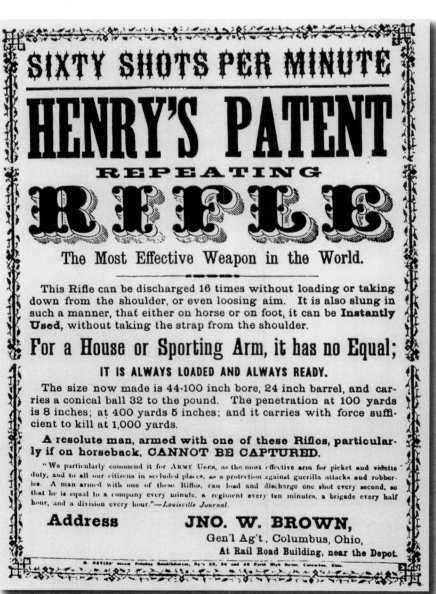

SIXTY SHOTS PER MINUTE

HENRY'S PATENT

REPEATING

RIFLE

The Most Effective Weapon in the World.

This Rifle can be discharged 16 times without loading or taking down from the shoulder, or even loosing aim. It is also slung in such a manner, that either on horse or on foot, it can be **Instantly Used**, without taking the strap from the shoulder.

For a House or Sporting Arm, it has no Equal;

IT IS ALWAYS LOADED AND ALWAYS READY.

The size now made is 44-100 inch bore, 24 inch barrel, and carries a conical ball 32 to the pound. The penetration at 100 yards is 8 inches; at 400 yards 5 inches; and it carries with force sufficient to kill at 1,000 yards.

A resolute man, armed with one of these Rifles, particularly if on horseback, CANNOT BE CAPTURED.

"We particularly commend it for ARMY USES, as the most effective arm for picket and vidette duty, and to all our citizens in secluded places, as a protection against guerilla attacks and robberies. A man armed with one of these Rifles, can load and discharge one shot every second, so that he is equal to a company every minute, a regiment every ten minutes, a brigade every half hour, and a division every hour."—*Louisville Journal.*

Address   JNO. W. BROWN,

Gen'l Ag't, Columbus, Ohio,

At Rail Road Building, near the Depot.

Winchester was a shrewd business man and his assessment was that the Volcanic loading system needed to be applied to a rifle rather than a pistol and that problems with the ammunition were also to blame for the gun's lack of success at that point. In a clever move he employed Benjamin Tyler Henry (1821-1898) as plant superintendent. Henry had gained his experience at the Springfield Armory and at Robbins and Lawrence. He was at the latter company when the Jennings Repeating Rifle was under development. Some of the features of this gun's reloading mechanism found their way through into the Volcanic system and subsequently into the Henry. By 1859, Henry had developed a .38 caliber rimfire brass cartridge to replace the earlier Volcanic caseless ammunition, where the powder charge was contained in the hollow base of the bullet. This system suffered from loss of gas and therefore power, whereas the brass cartridge expanded on firing to provide a better seal between the casing and the breech. However, tests showed that the .38 cal was too light and a heavier, more powerful .44 cartridge was perfected. Patented on October 16, 1860, the new rifle was named for its designer.

This in itself led to problems in the future, as it gave Henry proprietorial sway when it came to discussions about his pay with Oliver Winchester. After all, it was his gun; it was named after him!

Henry was hired at a salary of $1,500 per year in 1858 but under a contract scheme he was able to control and charge for the production with the

Above: An early, and very rare, iron-framed Henry.

Below: A cartridge box for the .44 Henry rim fire ammunition.

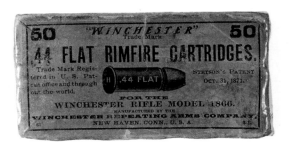

Below: This particular weapon, with serial #8794, has been identified as one of a batch issued to troops on guard duties in the area of Washington DC, in the latter part of the Civil War.

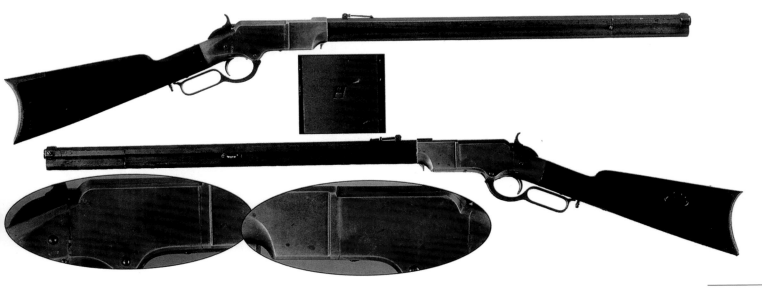

Above: Another brass frame Henry, this one carries the serial 788.

Below: The detail shows how a previous owner has fitted his own rear sight into a slot cut into the barrel, and which has been made from an "Indian head" penny.

management paying his materials and sales costs. This enabled him to make twice his salary. But even this scarcely rewarded him for developing the mechanism which ultimately made Winchester's fortune.

The resultant Henry Model 1860 was chambered for the .44 Henry rimfire cartridge, and had a fifteen-round, tubular magazine under the barrel. It had an octagonal 24-inch barrel with no foregrip, but with a walnut buttstock and a brass buttplate. Some 14,000 of these rifles were made between 1861 and 1866, of which the early examples had iron frames and the later guns a brass frame. When the ring trigger was pushed forward, the rearmost round in the magazine was forced into a scoop-shaped carrier by the magazine spring. The hammer was then cocked and the ring trigger drawn to the rear, which lifted the round into the chamber.

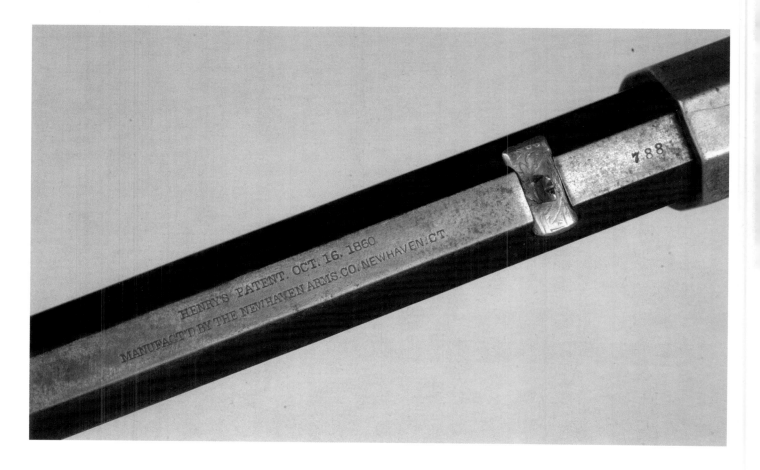

The Henry rifle represented some very significant advances, the most important being that the fifteen-round magazine gave the shooter a major increase in firepower. With the onset of the Civil War, the gun enjoyed much popularity and its rapid-fire qualities were much in demand. The South didn't have access to high-tech weapons of this kind, and the gun's prowess in certain battles like the siege of Atlanta gave the federal forces a big advantage. Advertising posters proclaimed a very bullish "sixty shots per minute" which, whether realistic or not, put it far ahead of the conventional muzzle-loading rifles of the time.

Above: Company A, 7th Illinois Color Guard, were tasked with defending Washington from Confederate attack. They were equipped with the fast-firing Henry rifle.

Ingram Mac 10

Type: Submachine gun	
Origin: Military Armament Corp.	
Caliber: .45	
Barrel length: 5.75 inches	

In the late 1940s gun designer Gordon Ingram set himself the goal of producing a very small, compact, and easy-to-manufacture sub-machine gun, which resulted in a series of weapons, starting with the Ingram Model 6 in 1949. Further work led to the Model 10, which was produced in various types between 1964 and the mid-1980s; approximately 16,000 were manufactured by a number of different companies and sold to the armed forces and police in several countries. The next weapon was the M11, which was similar in design to the M10 but slightly smaller and chambered for the 9 x 17mm Short cartridge. Although liked for its compactness, one of the major concerns by users of the Ingrams was their very high cyclic rate-of-fire: 1,500 rounds per minute with the M10 and 1,200 rpm in the M11.

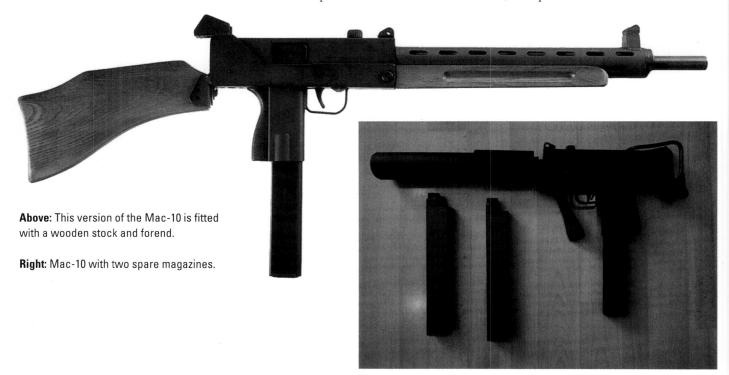

Above: This version of the Mac-10 is fitted with a wooden stock and forend.

Right: Mac-10 with two spare magazines.

The MAC-10 (*Military Armament Corporation Model 10*), officially the M-10, is a compact, blowback operated machine pistol that is chambered in either 45 ACP or 9mm. The prime factor in the gun's success was its two-stage suppressor designed by Mitchell Werbell III of Sionics for the MAC-10, which largely canceled the noise created, making it very quiet, to the point that the bolt could be heard cycling along with the suppressed report of the weapon's discharge; however, this was true only if subsonic rounds were used. The suppressor when used with a Nomex heatproof cover created a place to hold the firearm with the secondary hand, making it easier to control on fully automatic mode. This uniquely shaped suppressor gave the MAC-10 a very distinctive, if not aggressive appearance which also probably added to the gun's popularity. The term "MAC-10" is commonly used, but unofficial, parlance. Military Armament Corporation never used the nomenclature MAC-10 on any of its catalogs or sales literature, but because "MAC-10" became so frequently used by dealers, gun writers, and collectors, it became used more frequently than "M10" to identify the gun.

Above: The Mac-10 with a Nomex heat shield fitted to the suppressor.

Below: Mac-10 with a folding stock and extended barrel.

Bottom: John Wayne stars in the 1974 movie *McQ* along with the Mac-10.

During the 1970s the United States placed restrictions on the exportation of suppressors, and a number of countries canceled their orders of M-10s, as the effectiveness of the MAC-10's suppressor was one of its main selling points. This was one factor that led to the bankruptcy of Military Armament Corporation, another being the company's failure to recognize the private market. The original Sionics suppressor is 11.44 inches in length, 2.13 inches in overall diameter, and 1.20 pounds.

Due to its appearance and the reputation the open-bolt version gathered before the 1982 open-bolt ban, the semi-auto civilian version of the MAC-10, which operates differently than its military counterpart, became a target of the 1994 Assault Weapons Ban.

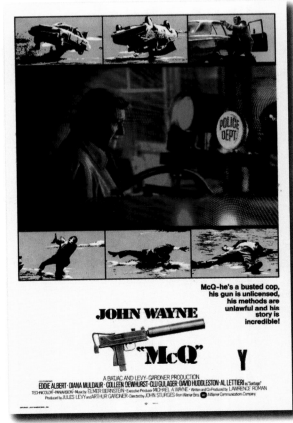

McQ-he's a busted cop, his gun is unlicensed, his methods are unlawful and his story is incredible!

JOHN WAYNE

"McQ"

A BATJAC AND LEVY-GARDNER PRODUCTION
EDDIE ALBERT · DIANA MULDAUR · COLLEEN DEWHURST · CLU GULAGER · DAVID HUDDLESTON · AL LETTIERI
TECHNICOLOR · PANAVISION · Music by ELMER BERNSTEIN · Executive Producer MICHAEL A WAYNE · Written and Co-Produced by LAWRENCE ROMAN
Produced by JULES LEVY and ARTHUR GARDNER · Directed by JOHN STURGES · from Warner Bros. A Warner Communications Company

M1 Carbine

Type: Semi-automatic carbine

Origin: Winchester Repeating Arms Co. plus contract manufacturers

Caliber: .30

Barrel length: 18 inches

Overall length: 35.6 inches

Weight: 5.8 lbs loaded (with sling)

As World War II loomed the United States ordnance department was advised that fighting techniques and conditions were going to be very different from the trench style combat experienced in the First World War. The likelihood of the use of more rapid deployment of enemy troops into the combat zone either by air or armored vehicle (exemplified by Germany's "Blitzkreig" tactics) gave rise to a call for U.S. troops to be armed with a handy carbine with semi-automatic fire capability. The existing 30-06 M2 military rifle was comparatively heavy and cumbersome. It was better suited for long range engagement from a fixed position than in a sudden fire fight. Although handguns like the M1911 semi-automatic pistol and the M1917 revolver could easily be carried in action, they lacked accuracy at longer range. The Thompson sub machine gun had the necessary firepower for a close fight, but it was heavy and unable to engage the enemy at distance. Major Rene Studler of the Ordnance Department reasoned that the best route was to use a scaled-down version of the Winchester M2 rifle. A design for the gun had already been

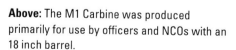

Above: The M1 Carbine was produced primarily for use by officers and NCOs with an 18 inch barrel.

Right: Jimmy Stewart starring as David Marshall Williams in the movie *Carbine Williams*.

submitted to Studler's department. He was looking to save weight from the rifle's seven-and-a-half pounds down to five pounds for the carbine.

The M2 was originally designed by Jonathan (Ed) Browning, the brother of John M. Browning. On Ed's death in 1939, Winchester brought in David Marshall Williams, who had developed a revolutionary new short stroke gas piston that he applied to the M2. The movie *Carbine Williams* starring James Stewart celebrates Williams' contribution to the creation of the carbine, turning him and the gun into a Hollywood legend. In actual fact the finished carbine had little in common with Williams' work on the M2 Rifle.

An experienced design team at Winchester had cobbled together a prototype carbine for Ordnance approval using sundry parts. These included Williams' short stroke piston, the M1 Garand Rifle's buttstock, its rotating bolt and operating slide, together with the trigger housing and lock mechanism from a Winchester 1905. The resulting firearm used lighter .30 caliber (7.62mm) ammunition, which provided a mid range muzzle velocity of 1970 feet per second. The lighter round was developed from the defunct Winchester .32 self-loading cartridge and had a round nose. This lighter ammunition meant that soldiers were able to carry more rounds.

Above: A poster for the movie that dates from 1953.

Left: A collection of items concerning the .30 ammunition used by the M1 carbine includes a 600-round metal canister, a cotton ammo pouch and a 10-round clip.

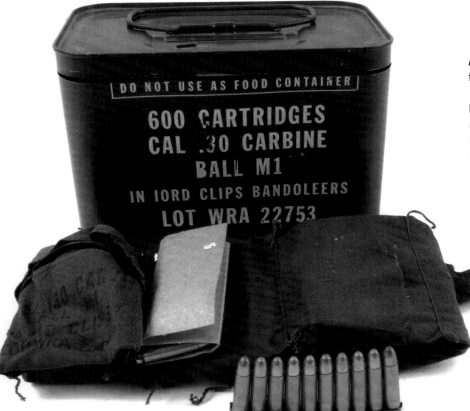

Top: This carbine has the commonly used canvas pouch strapped to the buttstock, which held two extra clips of ammunition.

Above: This paratroop version has a skeleton stock and pistol grip to save weight and increase maneuverability.

Various different types of magazines were used on the new gun. The most common of these carried fifteen rounds. A canvas pouch strapped to the buttstock contained two extra clips.

Approval for the carbine was quickly granted by the Ordnance Department. After further refinements by Winchester, production began. The first M2 was delivered in 1942 to U.S. troops involved in the European campaign.

Right: The M1 carbine was used widely as a support weapon. Here an NCO oversees two men on mortar detail.

M1 Carbine received mixed reviews in service. On the plus side, it was lightweight, had compact ergonomics, and delivered instant semi-automatic firepower. On the negative side, the gun's ultimate lack of stopping power became an issue in some combat theaters. Inevitably, no gun is a perfect all-rounder, but the M1 proved to be a useful weapon and remained in service from 1942 to 1973. Over six million examples were produced. The gun is also used as a hunting rifle by civilians and is employed by many security organizations worldwide.

Below: The carbine in the field. This one is fitted with a spike type bayonet for close combat.

M2 Machine Gun

Type: Heavy machine gun

Origin: Various U.S. arsenals

Caliber: 0.50in

Barrel length: 45.0 inches

Opposite page: The M2HB .50 caliber machine gun has an effective range of 2,000 yards, making it eminently suitable for marine applications.

Below: The M2 was used extensively during World War II, both by the United States and many other countries. It was also used in Korea, Vietnam, Somalia, the First Gulf War, the Second Gulf War, and continues to be in active service to this day.

The M2 was first introduced in 1933 and was originally intended for use on multiple anti-aircraft mounts. A version was also developed as a tank turret gun, and another for use with a ground mount. The guns worked on the well tested Browning system of short recoil. When the cartridge was fired, the barrel and breechblock (which securely locked together) recoiled for just under half an inch when the barrel was stopped by means of an oil buffer. At this stage, the pressure had dropped sufficiently for the breechblock to unlock and continue to the rear under the initial impetus given to it by the barrel, extracting and ejecting the empty case and extracting the next live round from the belt. Once the rearward action had stopped, the compressed return spring then took over and drove the working parts sharply forward, chambering the round, locking the breechblock, and firing the cartridge, after which the cycle continued as long as the trigger was pressed and there were rounds in the belt.

The gun would fire automatically only, though some were equipped with bolt latches to allow single rounds to be fired if necessary. Although this gun functioned well enough mechanically, it showed an unfortunate tendency to overheat, so that seventy or eighty rounds were about the maximum that could be fired continuously without a considerable pause to allow the barrel to cool. In practice, this was completely unacceptable, so a heavy barrelled version (the M2HB) was adopted. The extra metal in the barrel made a considerable difference and this new gun was most effective. Although both the gun and its cartridge were heavy, it was hugely successful as an extremely powerful automatic assault weapon, especially against aircraft, helicopters, and light vehicles.

M3A1 "Grease Gun"

Type: Submachine gun

Origin: Small Arms Development Branch

Caliber: .45

Barrel length: 8.0 inches

Early in World War II (1941), the Small Arms Development Branch of the United States Army Ordnance Corps set out to produce an inexpensive weapon that could be mass produced using modern methods. Once the basic design had been developed, a very detailed study of the methods that were used to manufacture the British Sten gun was undertaken. Development work was so speedy that prototypes had already been tested by the end of 1942. The new weapon was designated M3, and was a highly utilitarian arm. It was almost exclusively made from stampings, and only the barrel and bolt were machined.

The gun worked on the blowback method, and had no provision to fire single rounds. Its low cyclic rate made this acceptable. Its stock was of retractable wire, and it had a caliber of 0.45 inches, although it was easy to convert to 9mm. Its famous nickname came from its remarkable resemblance to a garage mechanic's grease gun. Large-scale use exposed some defects in the design of the gun, and several model simplifications were introduced. The revised version of the weapon was designated the M3A1. This gun also worked by blowback, but had no handle. Instead, the firer inserted a finger into the slot in the receiver, by which method the bolt could be withdrawn. The bolt had an integral firing pin. This was worked on guide rods, which made complicated finishing of the inside of the receiver unnecessary as they facilitated smooth functioning with very little interruption from dirt. An oil container was built

Above: The M3 was deliberately designed as a utilitarian weapon, making for quick and easy wartime production.

into the pistol grip and a small bracket was also added to the rear of the retractable butt. This acted as magazine filler. The gun had a box magazine that was not completely reliable in dirty or dusty conditions until the later addition of an easily removed plastic cover that eliminated this defect.

By the end of 1944, the new gun had officially replaced the Thompson as the standard submachine gun of the United States Army, a more powerful weapon than the Sten that had inspired its inception. A simple flash hider was added in 1945, which was held in place by a wing nut. Some examples of the gun were also fitted with silencers.

Above: Two Nazis held comfortably at bay with an M3 during the D-Day invasion.

The M14 Rifle

Type: Selective–fire rifle
Origin: National Armory, Springfield
Caliber: 7.62x51mm
Barrel length: 22 inches

The M14 rifle was the last American "battle rifle" (weapons that fire full-power rifle ammunition, such as the 7.62×51mm) to be issued in quantity to U.S. military personnel. After the M14's adoption, Springfield Armory began tooling a new production line in 1958, delivering the first service rifles to the U.S. Army in July 1959. It gradually replaced the M1 Garand in U.S. Army service by 1961 and in US Marine Corps service by 1965. The M14 rifle, officially the United States Rifle, 7.62 mm, M14, is an selective-fire automatic rifle that fires 7.62×51mm NATO (.308 Winchester) ammunition. It was the standard issue infantry rifle for U.S. military personnel in the Contiguous United States, Europe, and South Korea from 1959 until it was replaced by the M16 rifle in 1970. It was fortunate that the gun was indeed selective because with the M14's powerful 7.62×51 mm cartridge, the weapon was virtually uncontrollable in fully automatic mode. Most M14s were permanently set to semi-automatic fire only to avoid wasting ammunition in combat

The rifle served adequately during its brief tour of duty in Vietnam. Though it was unwieldy due to its length and weight, the power of the 7.62 mm NATO cartridge compensated by its extended range, allowing its fire to penetrate far in the dense jungle undergrowth. Glass fiber stocks were introduced to prevent loss of accuracy caused when the traditional wooden stocks swelled in the jungle humidity.

The rifle still remains in limited front line service within all branches of the U.S. military, being recognized as an accurate competition and sniping weapon. The Marine Corps returned the M14 to service during the Iraq and Afghanistan Wars. The 5.56 mm round proved inadequate for the type of

Below: The M14 was the last of the traditional American "battle rifles" being replaced by the M16.

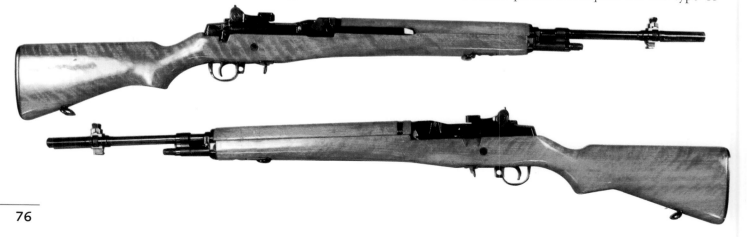

combat encountered and the Marines used the M14 to create the DMR (Designated Marksman Rifle). The DMR, being a modified version of the M14, is a semi-automatic, gas-operated rifle chambered for the heavier 7.62x51mm NATO cartridge.

The rifle continues to be used as a ceremonial weapon by honor guards, color guards, drill teams.

Above: A Navy Seal checks his modified M14. Note the foregrip for steadying the gun when undertaking sniper duties.

M60 Machine Gun

Type: Light machine gun

Origin: Saco Defence Inc., Saco, Maine

Caliber: 7.62 mm

Barrel length: 25.5 inches

The M60 was the first post-war light machine gun developed by the U.S. Army. It combined the best features of the German MG 42 and the FG 42 assault rifle.

The gun was largely manufactured from stampings, rubber, and plastics. It had a somewhat fussy, cluttered appearance and was afflicted by several basic problems. In the first place, there was no gas regulator: the supply of gas was fixed and could not be controlled by the firer. Under certain conditions the gun either stopped, or less usually "ran away." This means that the working parts of the gun go back far enough to feed, chamber, and fire another round, but not far enough to be engaged by the sear. This means that the gun may continue to fire even after the firer's finger has been lifted from the trigger. Although this was very disconcerting, the problem is by no means limited to the M60. The difficulty could be overcome by holding onto the belt, and

Below: The M60 in action on the firing range.

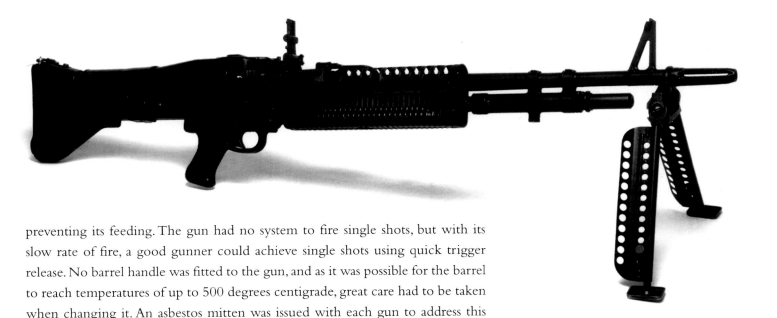

preventing its feeding. The gun had no system to fire single shots, but with its slow rate of fire, a good gunner could achieve single shots using quick trigger release. No barrel handle was fitted to the gun, and as it was possible for the barrel to reach temperatures of up to 500 degrees centigrade, great care had to be taken when changing it. An asbestos mitten was issued with each gun to address this problem, but these were frequently lost in action. In this case, the gunner could use a piece of rag.

One of the best features of the gun was its chromium-plated barrels, which had stellite liners for the first six inches of the chamber. The gun sights were adequate, but the zeroing system was not. A belt or box was supplied when the gun was being used on the move, and a simple, robust tripod was available for the sustained fire role.

The M60 was used extensively in the Vietnam War as a squad automatic weapon with many U.S. units. Every soldier in the rifle squad would carry an additional 200 linked rounds of ammunition for the M60, a spare barrel, or both. The up-gunned M113 armored personnel carrier ACAV added two M60 gunners beside the main .50 caliber machine gun, and the River Patrol Boats had one in addition to two .50 caliber mounts. During the action in Vietnam, the M60 was nicknamed "The Pig" due to its bulky size. Vietnam's tropical climate harshly affected weapons, and the M60 was no exception. Its light construction made the gun damage easily, and critical parts like the bolt and op rod wore out quickly. Even so, soldiers appreciated the gun's handling, mechanical simplicity, and effective operation from a variety of firing positions. Navy Seals used M60s with shorter barrels and no front sights to reduce weight further. The gun could also be used with feed chutes from backpacks to have a belt of thousands of rounds ready to fire without needing to reload.

This combat experience led to a considerably improved version of the gun that was issued as the M60E1, but many of its roles have now been assumed by the M249 (Minimi).

Marlin Model 1894

Type: Lever-action repeating rifle

Origin: Marlin Firearms Co, New Haven, Connecticut

Caliber: See text

Barrel length: 24-32 inches

Below: An original Model 1894 in .25-20 caliber with a 24-inch round barrel. The 1894 can be identified from the 1893 by its shorter action as seen here.

Bottom: A modern Model 1894CSS in stainless steel, chambered for 357 Magnum or .38 Special with a 9 shot tubular magazine. The carbine has an 18.5-inch barrel with deep-cut Ballard-type rifling, together with five machined solid steel forgings and a fancy checkered American black walnut straight-grip stock.

As far as the Western market went, Winchester didn't have it all their own way. The Marlin Firerams Company launched its first Lever-Action rifle in 1881. This was followed by the Model 1893, which was the company's first rifle designed for the recently introduced smokeless cartridges. It was offered in five calibers, while the barrels could be either round or octagonal, and varied in length between 24 and 32 inches. Some 900,000 were manufactured, which were marked "Model 1893" up to 1905, but this was shortened to "Model 93" thereafter. The Model 1894 was very similar to the Model 1893, but with a shorter action; the example seen here is in .25-20 caliber and has a 24-inch round barrel. Some 250,000 Model 1894s were produced between 1894 and 1935. Marlins were mass produced and were sold at competitive prices as they are today. As a result, many would have been a popular cowboy weapon.

In 1969 the company returned the popular Model 1894 to production, chambered for the .44 Magnum. Since then a wide variety of Model 1894s has appeared, chambered for rounds varying in caliber from .22 through .38 Special to this Model 1894 Cowboy, which is chambered for the .45 Long

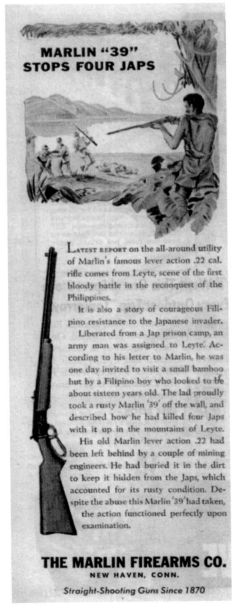

Colt round. This version was first marketed in 1996 and is intended to meet the requirements of the Cowboy Action Shooting sport. The weapon weighs 7.5 pounds and the tubular magazine holds ten rounds.

Mossberg Shotgun

Type: Slide-action shotgun

Origin: O.F. Mossberg & Sons Inc., North Haven, Connecticut

Caliber: 12 gauge

Barrel length: 18.5 inches

The Mossberg Model 500 pump-action shotgun has been in production for well over 20 years, during which time many millions have been sold. There have been at least seventeen variants, ranging from standard field models, through slug (including fully rifled), bantam for young shooters, turkey, waterfowl, security and combination models, and the gun has also been accepted by the U.S. army. The Model 500 is marketed in a wide variety of barrel lengths, calibers and finishes, and the standard magazine holds five shells.

Adopted by the United States Marine Corps in 1987, the Mossberg 590 is a ruggedized version of Mossberg's 500 series pump-action shotgun. Available in dozens of configurations, the 500 is the second most popular shotgun in

Right: A U.S. soldier in Iraq in 2004 with a Mossberg 500.

Above: The Mossberg 590A1 Tactical is a development of the Model 500.
It comes in 12 gauge and has a tactical flashlight, collapsible stock, and six-shot capability.

America, and one of the most dependable firearms ever made. Equally well-suited for hunting, home defense, or combat, the Mossberg 500 optimizes shotgun versatility. Its only downside is that it doesn't pair well with pistol-grip stocks, due to the location of its tang-mounted safety.

Above: Shown here is a Model 500 Crown Grade with 28.25-inch vent-ribbed barrel in 20 gauge.

Above: This one is in 12 gauge with a 28-inch vent-ribbed barrel and a Woodlands camouflage pattern finish.

Above: Finally we have a Model 500 ATP in 12 gauge, with plastic pistol grips and no stock butt.

The Plains Rifle

Type: Plains rifle

Origin: Various St. Louis gunmakers

Caliber: see text

Barrel length: see text

President Thomas Jefferson instigated the spirit of Westward expansion, seeking out the potential of the United States after the Louisiana Purchase in 1803. His intention was to consolidate the nation's grip on its newly acquired territories by exploring and laying claim to the land between St. Louis, known as the "gateway to the West," and ultimately the West Coast. In 1804 he commissioned Lewis and Clark to survey possible routes across the Rockies to unite the continents' East and West coasts. Because the explorers would naturally encounter hostile Indian tribes and dangerous wildlife, together with the need to provide food for their own larder, their choice of firearm would be crucial.

In the early days the explorers would have the use of flintlock long arms left

Above: A half-stock plains rifle by Horace E. Dimick of St Louis. It is .58 caliber with a heavy 32.5-inch barrel.

over from the War of Independence, guns like the Model 1803 Harpers Ferry flintlock rifle, or the Charleville musket originally supplied by the French. These eighteenth-century firearms were fine in their day but the design was becoming outdated in the nineteenth century. The Kentucky rifle and other American longrifles were also available, but were unsuitable due to their smaller bore and lack of power to stop larger game. The long barrels were also somewhat cumbersome when maneuvering around in the dense forests that cloak the foothills of the Rockies.

To satisfy the demand for larger bore accurate rifles, a number of enterprising gunsmiths set up shop in St. Louis from the early part of the nineteenth century onward. Two such men were Jacob and Samuel Hawken, who ran a gunshop from 1815 to 1858 in that city. Samuel and Jacob were trained by their father as gunsmiths back east. They moved west to supply guns right at the beginning of the Rocky Mountain fur trade. The brothers' claim to fame was the plains rifle produced in their shop. They designed and built a new kind of gun that combined the features that their customers needed in the west: a quality gun, light enough to carry all the time, capable of knocking down large game like buffalo at long range. These guns were named "Rocky Mountain Rifles," reflecting their clientele: the fur trappers, traders and explorers. The earliest known record of a Hawken rifle dates to 1823 when one was made for fur trader William Ashley. Each Hawken rifle was made

Below: A Classic two-pin half stock percussion plains rifle by S. Hawken, St. Louis.

Above and left: A Hawken shop Gemmer percussion plains rifle.

Opposite page: Joe Grandee's painting of a mountain man with his plains rifle.

Below: A heavy S.Hawken plains rifle made by Tristan Campbell, a partner of Sam Hawken.

individually by hand; no mass production methods were used. A number of famous frontiersmen were said to have owned Hawken rifles, including: Daniel Boone, Jim Bridger, and Kit Carson.

The Plains rifle had a shorter barrel than earlier rifles, such as the American Long Rifle, and the barrels were heavy and octagonal, bored out for large calibers—usually over .45. They were half stocked with curly maple and were required to have a high standard of finish such as ornate patch boxes, scrolled trigger guards, fancy hammers and engraved lock-plates. The investment in a quality rifle was considered worthwhile as it was often all that came between the owner and extinction in the wilderness. The Plains Rifle was therefore crucial to the early Westward expansion of the United States.

Horace E. Dimick also established a business in St. Louis in 1849, where he too produced Plains rifles. His guns were half stocked and had a heavy thirty-two-inch .58 caliber barrel, rifled according to the wording on his patent: "...by a system of straight grooves, extending from the base of the bore to about the position of the trunnions, and twisting thence to the muzzle."

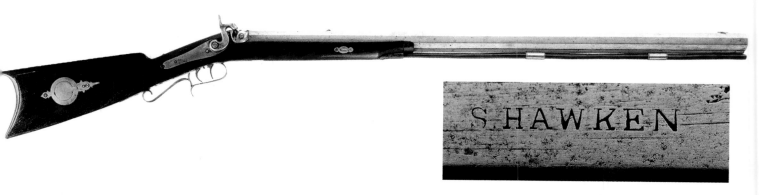

Remington Rolling Block Rifle

Type: Breech-loading rolling block rifle/carbine

Origin: E.Remington & Sons, Ilion, New York

Caliber: see text

Barrel length: see text

Remington continually acquired inventions and patents developed by others, and this one was to prove one of their most successful. The original concept for this style of breech-loader was devised by Leonard Geiger and developed by Joseph Rider, who took out joint patents with Remington in 1865.

Known as the split breech or "rolling block" system, it was simple to use, reasonably quick to operate, and extremely rugged and reliable. The firer simply had to pull back the hammer to cock it, then rotate the breech block downwards to open it and eject the spent case. A new round was loaded, then the block simply thumbed back upwards to lock the breech.

Rolling block arms quickly became popular and Remington eventually developed a bewildering array of service rifles, carbines, sporting guns and even pistols using the system. Many governments procured such weapons such as Mexico and Denmark although, surprisingly, the U.S. military never adopted it in a big way. The No.4 Rolling block was introduced in 1890 and became known as the "boy's rifle" becoming popular as a starter gun for young hunters and cadets. Almost 160,000 were produced by 1901, making it one of the most popular guns produced by any American manufacturer.

The rifle shown here was chambered for the government, 50-70 cartridge, and was actually manufactured by the Springfield Armory under license for the U.S. Navy. Many of these rifles were subsequently purchased for the French Army to use in the 1870-71 Franco-Prussian War.

A huge range of sporting, target, and hunting arms were also manufactured using the rolling block mechanism, and we show some examples here. These all use the first variant of the rolling block action, subsequently known as the No. 1 action.

Above: A close-up of the breech mechanism

Known as the No. 1 Sporting Rifle, this was made in a range of calibers, using both rimfire and centerfire cartridges, including .40, .44, .45, and .50 centerfire. Rimfire calibers include .44 and .46. Standard barrel lengths were twenty-eight inch and thirty inch.

This Sporting Rifle has been made with a much thicker, heavier barrel than standard.

Below: The Creedmoor rifle range on Long Island was established by the National Rifle Association to advance the standard of marksmanship in the U.S.

Creedmoor was the home of American precision long-range target shooting, and many rifle manufacturers used the name to denote specialized long-range target versions of their products. This one was known as the Long Range Creedmoor No. 1, and was chambered for .44–90, .44–100, and .44–105 necked and straight cartridges. It had a thirty-four inch barrel, a folding long-range sight on the "tang" (just above the wrist of the stock), a pistol grip shape to the stock, and a globe front sight.

In 1885 Remington offered this lighter and smaller version of the No. 1 action, with thinner receiver and less overall weight than the earlier design. It was intended for lower-powered ammunition, and was available in a range of calibers, including .22, 25, .32, and .38 rimfire, together with .32, .38, and .44 centerfire. The later No. 2 Remington was even lighter, with a smaller frame.

Below: Mexican "Rurales" were issued with Rolling Block carbines. Photo circa 1910.

Left: In 1913 Remington introduced a military-style rifle for Boy Scout use, based on the No. 4 action. The Remington No. 4S Boy Scout Rifle complete with leather sling strap, bayonet, and leather scabbard was offered for $8.

Below: After their merger in 1911, Remington and UMC made and actively marketed their own ammunition for their guns.

Right: General Custer headed an expedition into the Black Hills of Dakota in 1874. Very few white men had accessed these hills and returned alive. Custer was scouting them for the U.S. Army in order to establish an outpost there. He is photographed here with a Grizzly bear he shot, which he considered one of his finest kills. He is holding his favorite gun: a 50 caliber Remington Rolling block rifle. He wrote to the company praising the gun.

Remington Army Revolver

Type: Six-shot single-action revolver

Origin: Remington Armory, Ilion, New York.

Caliber: .44

Barrel length: 8 inches

Below: The Remington –Beals .44 Army Revolver.

It is an easy, but incorrect, assumption that all martial revolvers were Colts. In fact Remington produced a solid, reliable and popular revolver—the Model 1861—and thousands were made and used by both sides during the Civil War and after. Many were manufactured at the Remington facility at Utica created to meet the demands of the Civil War, although they bear "Remington, Ilion," markings.

It started with the Remington–Beals revolver and soon after that entered production, the company looked to improve the design. The main difference was a modification to the way the cylinder axle pin was retained. A channel was cut in the top of the rammer arm to allow the pin to be removed easily.

Above: Model 1861 Revolver

Right: New Model Army Revolver

Opposite page: A Union soldier poses with his Remington Model 1861.

The system was patented by a Dr. Elliott, and the weapon is sometimes referred to as the Model 1861 Elliott's Patent Army Revolver. In service conditions this system was found to be too fragile, and many revolvers had a small screw added to block this channel.

The Model 1861 is also known as the "Old Model Army." It was specified by the Ordnance Department in .44 caliber. It had a distinctive outline, with an integral top strap, large gap in front of the lower edge of the cylinder, and a long sloping web on the loading ram under the barrel. This form set the pattern for all subsequent Remington military percussion revolvers. The top strap gave the gun an extra rigidity that Colt revolvers of the period didn't have.

Wartime experience showed up some weaknesses in Remington's Model 1861, especially concerning the cylinder fixing system. So in late 1862, Remington modified the design by improving the fixing pin and adding safety notches around the rear edge of the cylinder. The first improved New Models were delivered in March 1863. The end result was one of the finest percussion revolvers ever, and the only one to really challenge Colt's dominance of the military market. Over 120,000 were delivered during the Civil War, and at its peak, production reached over 1,000 a week.

Of course, a version of the New Model was made in .36 Navy caliber, but this didn't sell quite so well—although the 28,000 produced was still a healthy number.

Remington Model 12 Slide-Action Rifle

Type: Slide-action repeating rifle

Origin: Remington Arms Co., Ilion, New York

Caliber: .22S, .22L, .22LR, .22 Remington

Barrel length: 22 inches

Another designer who worked with Remington was John D. Pedersen, who in 1907 designed this slide-action .22 rifle, which eventually become known as the Remington Model 12. Closely resembling a slide-action shotgun, the Model 12 used a similar under-barrel tubular magazine to hold the cartridges. It became one of the best selling sporting rifles ever, with over 831,000 made in a twenty-seven year period from 1909 to 1936. It was a first gun for many Americans and became familiar to all who had their first shot at a shooting gallery at a county fair. While all Model 12s fired .22 rounds, they came chambered for a range of cartridges, with the magazine capacity varying from ten to fifteen with the size of the cartridge. The first rifle shown is a Model 12 with grooved underbarrel slide.

Below: The Model 12B Gallery special came with a 24-inch barrel and extended magazine for 25 .22 Short cartridges

Below: This Model 12 has a factory-engraved receiver and rounded understock grip.

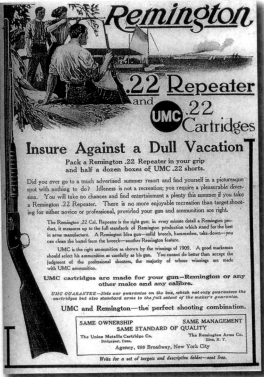

Left and above: Posters designed to attract young buyers of their popular rifles were handed out to hardware stores and other outlets by Remington.

Richmond Rifles

Type: Percussion rifle

Origin: Richmond Armory, Richmond, Virginia

Caliber: .58

Barrel length: 40 inches

Below: Richmond's Tredegar Iron Works was a major center for iron and steel casting and forging for the Confederacy during the Civil War.

At the outset of the Civil War the Confederacy realized that they needed to secure a source of mass armament for their troops. The industrial North had plenty of capacity for rifle production and the main Springfield arsenal was situated safely well away from access by the Confederacy. However during the Confederate raid on the more vulnerable Harpers Ferry Armory in April 1861, captured parts and gunmaking equipment were moved to Richmond, Virginia and Fayetteville, North Carolina to begin production of rifles and muskets. The Richmond Armory produced thousands of weapons from 1861 to 1865, in larger numbers than any other Confederate longarm. Most were based on the Model 1855 and 1863 rifles.

Confederate production didn't use the Maynard system, but as the captured

Above and below: This rifle has the "high hump" lockplate, and is dated 1862. The detail shows "J.W. Cool" and "10 VA" carved into the butt. Private Jacob Cool was killed at Chancellorsville on May 3, 1863.

lockplate dies were set for the Model 1855 and its Maynard Tape primer lock, consequently early Richmond lockplates followed the same shape. This gave an unusually high hump where the primer system would have been. Rifles to this design are usually referred to as Type I and Type II and many minor variations exist.

Left: The Bellona Foundry was near Richmond and ranked second as a major arms production unit after Tredegar.

Above: Later modifications produced the Type III, recognized by the lower hump on the lockplate. The one shown here is dated 1862, and the butt is carved with "James Clay 18 Virginia" and an array of 13 stars.

Left: James Clay is known to have served in Company G of the 18th Virginia and participated in "Pickett's Charge" at Gettysburg.

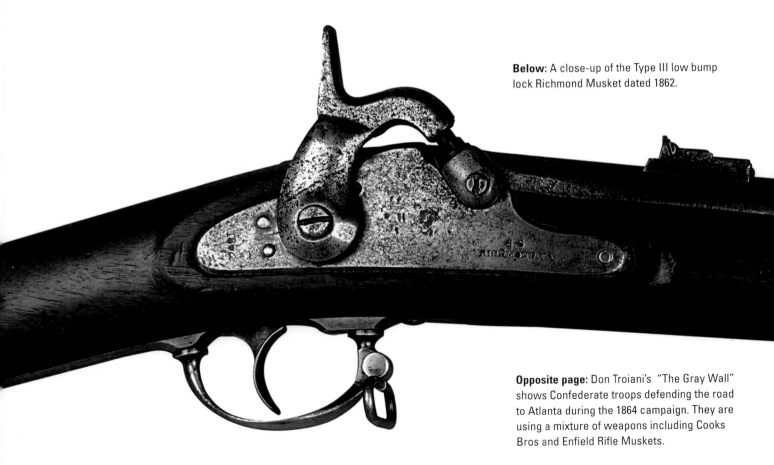

Below: A close-up of the Type III low bump lock Richmond Musket dated 1862.

Opposite page: Don Troiani's "The Gray Wall" shows Confederate troops defending the road to Atlanta during the 1864 campaign. They are using a mixture of weapons including Cooks Bros and Enfield Rifle Muskets.

Ruger M14 Carbine

Type: Semi-automatic carbine
Origin: Sturm, Ruger & Co, Southport, Connecticut
Caliber: .223 Remington
Barrel length: 18.5 inches

The Mini-14 was first introduced in 1974 by Ruger as a paramilitary-style semi-automatic carbine. It had an 18.5-inch barrel, was chambered for the .223 Remington round, and used a gas-operated action. It was originally sold with either five, ten, or twenty round magazines, but the two larger magazines are now available to law-enforcement agencies only. The name Mini-14 is derived from the military M14 rifle implying a miniature version of the M14. Ruger used the M14 as a model for the new gun while incorporating numerous innovations and cost-saving engineering changes. The Mini-14 proved popular with small-game hunters, ranchers, law enforcement agencies, security personnel, and target shooters. During its 40-plus year life it has become an American Classic.

Ranch Rifle

In 1982 Ruger began marking many Mini-14 rifles with "RANCH RIFLE" instead of "Mini-14" on the receiver. This version was optimized for use with a telescope sight and thus was produced with integral scope bases on receiver and was supplied from the factory with Ruger scope rings. The rifle's ejector is set to eject the spent cartridge case at a lower angle to avoid hitting the low-mounted scope and the rear sight has a folding aperture, which fits under the scope. The older models lacked a winged front sight. The Ranch Rifles are fairly basic models, generally coming with a wood rifle stock or synthetic stock with black or stainless receiver, and feature the standard 18.5-inch tapered barrel. The NRA edition favors a 16-inch barrel. The rifle feature an adjustable ghost ring rear sight and winged front sight. They are sold with a 20 round detachable magazine; however in some states like New York, New Jersey, and California where high capacity magazines are illegal, the rifles are sold with 5 round magazines instead. This model will chamber both .223 Remington and

Below: Ruger Mini-14 Ranch Rifle with synthetic stock chambered for .223 Remington.

5.56x45mm NATO ammunition. Later developments of the Mini-14 range are the Mini Thirty rifles, and Deerfield Carbines. The Mini Thirty rifle is chambered for 7.62x39mm and is designed for small and medium-sized game. The Deerfield Carbine is chambered in .44 Magnum, and features a flush-mounted four-round detachable rotary magazine. It is designed for deer hunting in close cover. All Ranch Rifles and Mini Thirty rifles come fitted with scopes from the factory.

Schoyen Target Rifles

Type: Single-shot rifle	
Caliber: .32 .40	
Barrel length: 30 inches	
Stock: Walnut, checkered	

Below: This Remington has been converted to under-lever action by Carlos Gove, the pioneer Gun-maker of Denver, and has double set triggers. Carlos Gove rebuilt guns using this technique from 1873-77. The gun was handed down through a western family for several generations, having been given to Charlie Robbie, the original owner, for killing an Indian at the Sand Creek Massacre.

During the 1870s there was a rise in interest in long-range single-shot rifle target shooting in the German schuetzen style. One famous example of schuetzen shooting took place at the Long Range Black Powder match in 1874 at Creedmoor in Queens, New York. The competition was between the United States and Ireland and was held at the National Rifle Association's newly established shooting facility, which had been built on the site of the Creed farm. The land around this area reminded many of the moorland in Great Britain, hence the term "Creedmoor."

The shooters adopted various positions, including lying on their backs and standing straight up. This close interest in target shooting provided America with the foundations of its skill with weapons that paid off in two World Wars.

To cater to the increasing interest in schuetzen shooting various gunmakers and gun customizers began to produce guns for this style of shooting. These included a group of gunmakers who were based around Denver, Colorado and specialized in fancy modified single-shot rifles.

The Denver gunmakers based much of their output on the successful single-shot rifles of the day, including the Remington Rolling Block, the Sharps Model 1874, and Winchester's High and Low Wall target-shooting rifles (designed by John Browning).

Gunmakers such as Carlos Gove, J.P Lower, and George C. Schoyen were part of a thriving western firearms industry that specialized in producing schuetzen type rifles. Some of these gunsmiths had German roots and their skills came from the German tradition. After losing everything in the Great Chicago Fire of 1871, George C. Schoyen relocated to Denver, Colorado, where he established his gunshop and quickly gained a reputation for manufacturing accurate barrels. In fact he is now regarded as one of the finest barrel makers of the mid to late-nineteenth century. He was also a very competent target shooter and regularly competed in the area's shooting matches. His personal Winchester Model 1885 is shown below.

This Sharps Model 1874 receiver is marked with the two line 1869 patent date on the left side and the serial number is marked on the upper tang. The rifle is fitted with a George Schoyen barrel. The top of the barrel is marked "GEO. SCHOYEN DENVER COLO." The barrel has a globe front sight and two filled dovetail slots (one near the front sight, one near the breech). The barrel and frame juncture is engraved. The upper tang has two holes tapped for the sight mounting. The action has a single plain trigger and the lever latch has been removed. It's mounted on a smooth forearm and has a checkered pistol grip stock with cheek piece and brass Schuetzen style buttplate.

Above: A Sharps Model 1874 modified by George C. Schoyen.

Oposite page: George C. Schoyen in his Denver Workshop.

Remington-Walker-Schoyen Hepburn Schuetzen rifle

This is a very fine example of the classic Schuetzen rifle. It is a Remington Walker with a Schoyen barrel. The octagonal barrel is 30 inches long and marked "Geo C. Schoyen, Denver, Colo." The gun has rear vernier sights, a front peep sight, and double set triggers with a ornate schuetzen style scrolled trigger-guard underlever.

Above and below: Examples of Schoyen's art: guns prepared to a very high standard of workmanship.

Sharps Carbines and Rifles

Type: Single shot, breech-loading carbine/rifle

Origin: Sharps Rifle Manufacturing Company, Hartford, Connecticut

Caliber: see text

Barrel length: see text

With unrest in the South and the seeds of war germinating, many arms manufacturers were seeking faster-loading weapons. The breech-loading mechanism had already been invented, as we have seen from the entry on Hall Breech-loaders, but that particular system failed on power loss due to the problems of sealing the breech.

Christian Sharps set up his company that same year and while Robbins & Lawrence made the guns, Sharps provided the technical advice and marketing support from the Sharps Rifle Manufacturing Co in Hartford, Connecticut. He specialized in a range of large caliber single-shot breech-loading rifles and carbines that were to be heavily used by soldiers in the Civil War and afterwards by sportsmen and hunters.

The popular Sharps rifle used a falling block breech design by Rollin White of the R&L Co. known as the knife-edge breech block, as well as the self-cocking device for the "box-lock" Model 1851.

This was known as the Second model, which used the Maynard tape primer, a system that fed a tape of priming caps to the hammer. This same system was used on Springfield muzzle-loading rifles such as the Model 1855 Rifle Musket. In 1851 the Model 1851 was brought to the Robbins & Lawrence Company of Windsor, Vermont where it was developed for mass production. This is referred to as the "First Contract," which was for 10,000 Model 1851 carbines—of which approximately 1,650 were produced by R&L in Windsor.

The Model 1852 was a neat saddle ring carbine that used a pellet primer mechanism in place of the Maynard system. The pellets were held in a slanting magazine attached to the breech sideplate and the pellets were fed up to the

Below: The Sharps Box lock Model 1851 was the forerunner of the later guns.

Above: Two early examples of the Sharps Model 1852 Saddle Ring carbine with the slant breech.

hammer as the trigger was released. Some 5,000 units were manufactured, these two being early guns numbered in the 2,600–3,950 range.

The New Model Carbine used the experience gained from the Model 1852 to update the rifle to what is known as the straight breech type. The Sharps patent primer system is now integral to the lockplate. Of this, some 98,000 were made of models 1859,1863, and 1865 although they can be regarded as a single type. The Model 1863, shown here below, was produced both with and without the patch box (twice as many without). The furniture changed from brass to iron and the sling ring bar on the carbine was shorter (the earlier longer designs had often

Below: The Sharps New Model Carbine shown from both sides with inset details.

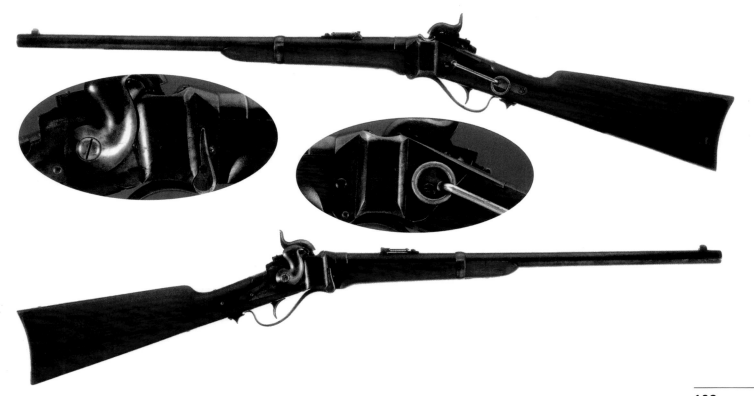

Above: An example of a Sharps NM 1859 breech-loading rifle, as issued to Berdan's Sharpshooters. Original guns like this one are hard to find.

snapped). Most of the output of this classic gun was in the hands of the Union troops, but the State of Georgia managed to acquire 2,000 for its cavalry and infantry from the first production of the 1859 model, which retained its brass furniture. Ironically by the time these successful weapons had been

Above: Hiram Berdan led his brigade of Sharpshooters through the Civil War using Sharps rifles.

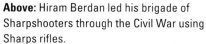

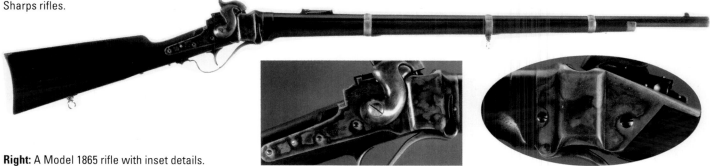

Right: A Model 1865 rifle with inset details.

developed, Christian Sharps had severed his relationship with the company that bore his name and and had formed a partnership with William Hankins.

Following the Civil War many guns were adapted for use on the Frontier. This is where the rifle version gained its nickname as the Sharps Buffalo Gun due to its large caliber and accuracy in bringing down this large animal in thousands.

Top: Sharps Model 1874 Sporting Rifle. This type of gun was popular with the hunters of buffalo and the gun acquired the nickname the "Sharps Buffalo Gun."

Above Sharps produced three new weapons in 1853: a military carbine, a military rifle with a longer barrel, and the sporting rifle, seen here. A total of 13,500 of all types were made between 1854 and 1858. The sporting rifle has a 25.5-inch barrel.

Left: Two hunters rest their Sharps rifles against the flank of a dead buffalo. With the advent of high powered and accurate rifles like the Sharps, hunters were able to decimate the herds of buffalo in a few short years.

Smith & Wesson Model 2 Army Revolver

Type: Six-round, service revolver

Origin: Smith & Wesson, Springfield, Massachusetts

Caliber: .32 rimfire

Barrel length: 4 inches, 5 inches and 6 inches

Opposite page: An unknown Union officer with a Model 2 in his belt

After their success with the Volcanic Pistol, in 1858 Horace Smith and Daniel Wesson (along with many others) took advantage of the expiry of Colt's master patent and began manufacture of their own revolver design. Smith and Wesson were one step ahead of the others though, in that having purchased Rollin White's patent for a bored-through cylinder, they were able to corner the market for cartridge revolvers.

Their Model 1 was a neat, light personal defense weapon firing a .22 rimfire cartridge. The more powerful Model 2 Army was a straightforward development of the Model 1, and Smith and Wesson had the good fortune that it became available just as the Civil War broke out. Important to this success was that it fired self-contained .32 rimfire cartridges, which were not affected by climate or humidity, and it was light enough to be carried as a back-up to rifle or saber. Thus, it was the very latest design and became an immediate success with Union troops, resulting in a huge backlog of orders for the company. The Model 2 had a six-round, fluted cylinder, was chambered for the .32 rimfire round, and was available with four-, five-, or six-inch barrels. Over 77,000 were sold between 1861 and the end of production in 1874.

Above: Despite its no-frills appearance, the Smith and Wesson Army was an immediate success.

Right: The six-round cylinder was chambered for metal rimfire cartridges.

Right: A handsome pair of Model 2 revolvers in their original case. Many Civil War soldiers self-purchased these weapons.

Opposite page: A Union officer fires his Smith and Wesson Army revolver into the melée at Alatoona Pass. In the background Union troops are firing their Henry rifles.

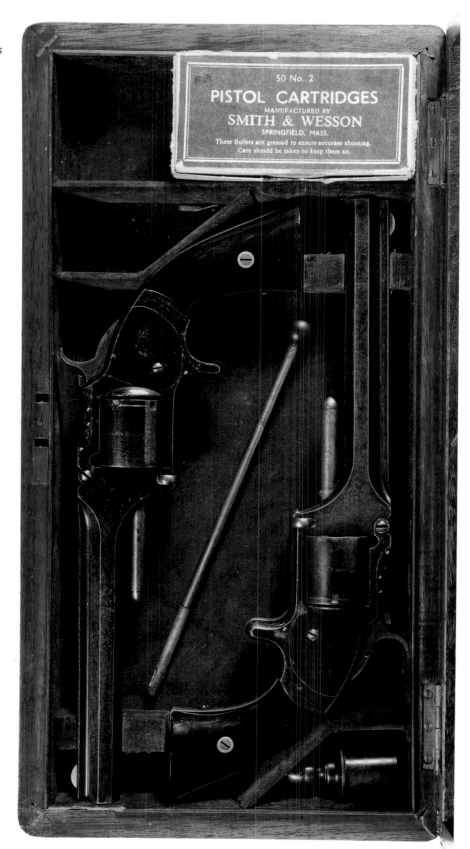

Smith & Wesson Model 3

Type: Six-round, hinged-frame, single-action revolver

Origin: Smith & Wesson, Springfield, Massachusetts

Caliber: .45 S&W

Barrel length: 7 inches

After the Civil War hostilities ended, the demand for guns slumped to an all-time low. Smith & Wesson began to look overseas for sales opportunities. The company obtained a large order from the Russian military authorities for the Smith & Wesson Model 3. Consequently the gun was nicknamed the "Russian." The model helped to establish the company as one of America's premier firearms makers. The Model 3 was used very widely in the West and was favored by lawman such as Wyatt Earp and outlaws like Jesse James. The United States Army adopted the Model 3. In this context, the gun was called the "Schofield," named after Major George Schofield. Schofield incorporated several design improvements into the gun that were based on his experience of using the gun in the field. As a result the weapon was extremely practical and reliable and was used throughout the Indian Wars of the West.

Schofield Model

The Model 3 was a major success for the company and inspired many variations, one of the most interesting being the Schofield Model. Major George Schofield of the U.S. Cavalry liked the Model 3 Smith & Wesson, but

Below: Model 3 first and second models.

patented a number of improvements designed to make it easier to use on horseback and, in particular, to reload while holding the reins. His proposals were accepted and in 1875 a government order for what was now designated the Model 3 Schofield was placed. In essence, Schofield's improvements included a modified barrel catch, improved extraction, and a barrel reduced to seven inches. A new round, the .45 Smith & Wesson (which was not interchangeable with the .45 Colt), was also developed for this weapon.

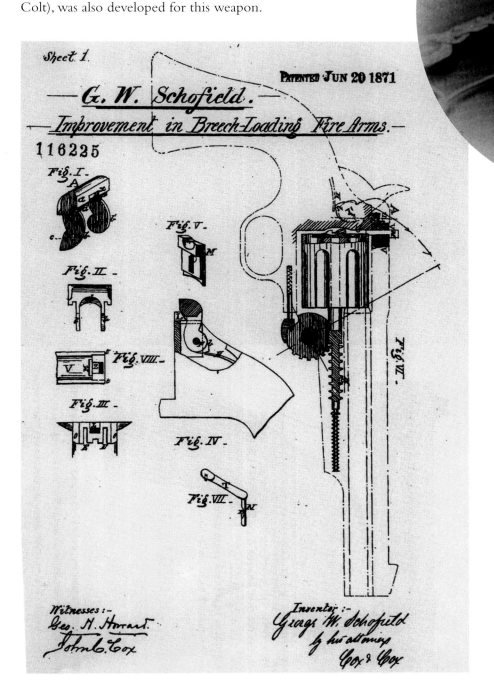

Above: Major George Schofield

Left: The patent forms containing Schofield's improvements, which included a modified barrel latch, improved extraction, and reduced barrel length.

Right: Russian Cossacks. The man on the left has a Smith & Wesson Russian model in his belt. The trigger spur is securing the gun in position.

Major Schofield's heavy revolver proved very popular with users, particularly in the cavalry, but by this time the Colt Single-Action Army was so well established that it stood no chance of long-term adoption and the Army discarded it after some 9,000 had been made. Army stocks were sold off in 1887, some going to National Guard units, some to Wells Fargo (with barrels shortened to five inches), and the balance to civilian arms dealers, many of which then found their way to the Western frontier. According to historians of the period, Schofields were carried by outlaws such as Frank and Jesse James and Bill Tilghman.

The Model 3 series was one of the most successful revolvers Smith and Wesson produced, and included a bewildering array of sub-types and variations to the basic design. In 1871 the Russian Government selected the Model 3 to re-equip their army, and once it was modified to take the Russian .44 necked cartridge, some 130,000 revolvers were delivered over the next 8 years.

Smith and Wesson also used the Russian cartridge in commercial weapons, and many thousands were sold, both on the U.S. domestic market and to overseas governments. Smith and Wesson "Russians" were adopted in various quantities by Turkey, Japan, Australia, Argentina, Spain, England, and others.

Above: An article in Scientific American featuring the Model 3

Left: The Russian Model with its distinctive trigger spur. It is thought that many of these were ground off for use in the U.S.

Smith & Wesson Model 29

Type: Six-round, solid-frame double action revolver

Origin: Smith & Wesson, Springfield, Massachusetts

Caliber: .44 Magnum

Barrel length: see text

When Clint Eastwood as Dirty Harry asked his quarry "Do you feel lucky?" as he pointed his .44 Magnum and asserts that he is armed with the most powerful handgun in the world that could "blow his head clean off," he made the Model 29 into a cult firearm. Originally introduced in 1956 to take advantage of the newly designed Smith & Wesson .44 Magnum round, the gun was undoubtedly one of the most powerful production handguns in the world and with an empty weight of 47 ounces, also one of the heaviest. The weight, however, was useful in suppressing the gun's recoil. It was originally available with 4 and 6.5-inch barrels with an 8.4-inch barrel option

Below: The Model 29-6 has a blue finish, 5-inch barrel, unfluted cylinder, and rubber grips.

Above: The Model 629 is mechanically identical, but is normally finished in satin-chrome. The one we show here has a 6-inch barrel and is finished in stainless steel.

being added in 1957. This version was popular with big game hunters who favored a handgun.

A 5-inch barrel version was briefly available during 1958, but only 500 were produced.

The popularity of the Dirty Harry movies, beginning in 1972, did much to promote both the gun and Clint's career, and Smith & Wesson were inundated with orders for the Model 29.

Many people who bought the gun on its reputation and looks were, in fact, often scared to use it because of its loud report and heavy kick. The model was later offered with a port on the top of the muzzle to vent some gases in order to subdue the recoil. This however only served to increase the gun's report.

The Model 29 showed that a revolver could still be counted as an effective weapon over 100 years after it was first widely used.

Above: This Model 29-4 has a 4-inch barrel and unfluted cylinder.

Belowt: THe Smith & Wesson Model 629 Performance Centre, a competition oriented variant with a weighted barrel for reducing recoil.

Left: Clint Eastwood as Dirty Harry points his Smith & Wesson Magnum with determination.

Spencer Repeating Carbine

Type: Magazine–fed repeating carbine

Origin: Spencer Rifle Co., Boston, Massachusetts

Caliber: .56-.56

Barrel length: 22 inches

Below: Christpher M. Spencer

Below right: Union troops with their Spencer Carbines.

Christopher M. Spencer first made his weapons at South Manchester, Connecticut, before moving to Boston in about 1862. By that time he had already designed a successful repeating rifle and carbine, the latter of which is described here. This gun was definitely one of the most charismatic, successful, and instantly recognizable weapons of the Civil War, and was so well received that it was personally endorsed by President Lincoln after he witnessed a field trial.

The gun is loaded via a tubular magazine housed in the buttstock, and rounds are fed into the breech by cranking down the trigger guard lever. Many soldiers were also equipped with the Blakeslee Cartridge Box, a wooden box containing between six and thirteen metal tubes pre-loaded with seven rounds. By placing the end of the reloading tube against the open end of the tubular magazine and dropping the cartridges through, the carbine could be reloaded in a matter of seconds.

The Spencer fired a .52 caliber rimfire straight copper cartridge. The case was actually .56 inches in diameter, so the cartridge is often referred to as the No. 56 or the .56-56.

We show several original examples of the 1860 and 1861 models. In an age

when many of the troops on the opposing side still carried muzzle-loaders, consider the advantages of being issued with a seven-shot repeating weapon. One Confederate Soldier captured at Gettysburg by Custer's Spencer-armed 5th Michigan Cavalry exclaimed, "[Spencers] load in the morning and fire all day."

Spencer also produced a later Model 1865, chambered for a .50 cartridge and with a slightly shorter twenty-inch barrel. Many were also fitted with the Stabler cut-off, a device which blocked the magazine. If accurate fire was needed, the user could block the magazine and feed single cartridges in to the breech, one at a time. The magazine could thus be kept full until rapid fire was needed, whereupon the firer simply slid the cut-off aside and let loose. Spencers continued to be used in the Indian Wars and on the Frontier for many years after the Civil War.

Below: Various examples of 1860 and 1861 models.

Following pages: The 1st Maine Cavalry in action during the Battle of Middleburg in 1863 with their Spencer carbines. Painted by Alfred R. Waud.

Spiller & Burr Revolver

Type: Six-round, percussion revolver

Origin: Spiller & Burr, Atlanta, Georgia

Caliber: .36

Barrel length: 7 inches

At the outbreak of the Civil War, the South stood at an immense disadvantage due to the underdeveloped condition of its munitions industry. There was no shortage of high-grade materials or skilled armaments workers in the North, but the Confederacy was short of both. Up to the outbreak of the Civil War, the South bought most of its weaponry from Northern manufacturers or from overseas (mainly Europe). But by 1862, it was obvious that the Confederate states needed their own armory to produce a plentiful supply of standardized weapons. The Confederate government appointed James H. Burton as its Superintendent of Armories. Burton was a trained engineer whose task was to make the Central Southern Armory a reality.

Originally, the factory was planned for Atlanta, but the high cost of real estate and the excessive cost of living for the workforce ruled out this location. By contrast, Macon offered Burton forty-seven acres of land, free of charge. By the standards of the time, the National Armory building was impressive. Designed by local civil engineer Augustus Schwaab, the main building was over 625 feet by 40 feet, and two stories high. It had twin towers at each end of the building, and a central bell tower that was four stories high. Building materials were imported from all over the South, including 1,280 cubic feet of dressed granite from Stone Mountain, Georgia, 5,000 barrels of lime (for cement), nine million bricks, three quarters of a million feet of board lumber, cast iron columns and ventilators weighing 40,000 pounds, innumerable doors and window frames, and a gigantic number of roofing slates.

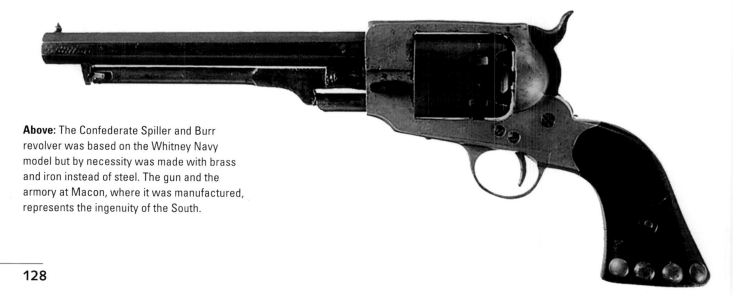

Above: The Confederate Spiller and Burr revolver was based on the Whitney Navy model but by necessity was made with brass and iron instead of steel. The gun and the armory at Macon, where it was manufactured, represents the ingenuity of the South.

The factory was an ambitious project for any government, let alone one fighting a costly war. The final bill for its construction rose to a staggering $1.2 million. Despite this bullish investment, the full manufacturing potential of the factory was never realized. Sherman's threatening presence meant that by 1864, most of the CSA machinery had to be evacuated from Macon to avoid capture by the Union.

Ultimately, the Confederate quest to be self-sufficient in weapons manufacture proved impossible. It is estimated that, in the course of the war, fewer than 10,000 revolvers were produced by all of the Southern armories combined. The vast majority of Confederate weapons were either imported or captured on the battlefield. The Spiller and Burr revolver was produced at the factory, and did in fact see military service. The revolver was originally part of a government contract for 15,000 guns. The Spiller and Burr had already been produced at facilities in Richmond and Atlanta before being manufactured at Macon. Colonel James H. Burton himself oversaw production of the gun, and an estimated 689 examples were manufactured at the new armory. Like many weapons manufactured in the South, the gun was based on an existing patent, in this case, the Whitney Navy model. The Confederacy was obliged to adapt the gun for Southern production, as materials were in short supply. Burton's factory made the cylinder out of cast iron instead of steel, and the frame from brass instead of iron. Although the gun strongly resembled the Whitney, it had a poorer standard of finish. Despite this, it was probably just as effective as its Northern counterpart.

Springfield Model 1861 Rifle

Type: Percussion rifle musket

Origin: National Armory, Springfield, Massachusetts

Caliber: .58

Barrel Length: 40in

Below: The National armory at Springfield is now a museum.

The city of Springfield, Massachusetts, formed the hub for military firearms manufacture from 1777 until 1968. It first came to prominence during the American Revolutionary War when George Washington approved the site as the emerging nation's primary arsenal. The armory was important as it pioneered groundbreaking techniques such as interchangeable parts and the assembly line method of mass production, and introduced modern business practices like hourly wages. The longarms produced here from 1794 to 1968 were known as Springfield Rifles. The armory is also a museum housing one of the largest collections of American military firearms.

At the outset of the Civil War there was a need for mass arms to arm the federal army, and the Model 1861 was a prime example of the efficiency of the national Armory in providing weapons in the face of emergency. The plentiful supply of weapons became a critical factor in overcoming the Confederacy.

Over one million of this percussion rifle were produced during the Civil War years, and together with its British Enfield counterpart they armed over forty percent of the fighting men in that conflict. This "Springfield Rifle" was well-balanced, reasonably light, reliable, and deadly effective in the right hands. Unlike the Model 1855 it no longer made use of the Maynard system, but instead relied on more conventional separate brass primer caps.

Thousands of Model 1861s were also made by individual contractors, and a selection are shown here.

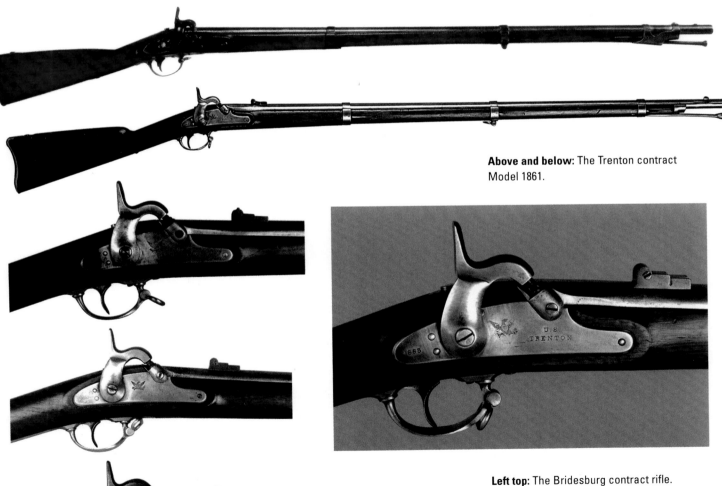

Above and below: The Trenton contract Model 1861.

Left top: The Bridesburg contract rifle.

Left middle: A Parker's Snow rifle.

Left bottom: A Model 1861 manufactured by Jenks.

SPRINGFIELD MODEL 1861 RIFLE

Left: The Provost Guard of the 107th Colored Infantry at Fort Corcoran, Washington DC with their Springfield Model 1863 Rifle muskets.

The Springfield Allin Trapdoor Rifle

Type: Breech-loading, single-shot cartridge rifle

Origin: National Armory, Springfield Massachusetts

Caliber: .45-70

Barrel length: 37 inches

By the end of the Civil War, the U.S. Army had realized that the infantry urgently needed a breech-loading rifle, but funds were also needed to rebuild the country after the devastation of war and government funds were short. In addition, there was a huge surplus of muzzle-loaders left over from the war. This problem was overcome by Edwin S. Allin, the Master Armorer at the Springfield Armory who devised and patented the "trapdoor" mechanism where the weapon was opened by means of a front-hinged lifting block on the top of the breech, which was raised to enable a new round to be loaded. Some 30,000 existing rifles and carbines were modified in what was known as the "Allin conversion," but once that program had been completed new rifles and carbines were designed from scratch incorporating the Allin "trapdoor." The first of these was the U.S. Model 1868, which was followed by the Models 1873, 1879, 1880, 1884 and 1889, each of which incorporated only minor changes over its predecessor.

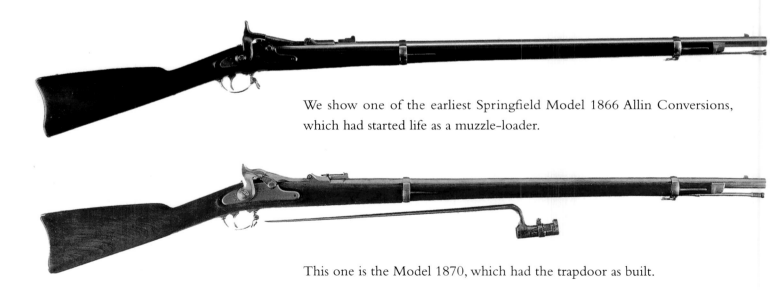

We show one of the earliest Springfield Model 1866 Allin Conversions, which had started life as a muzzle-loader.

This one is the Model 1870, which had the trapdoor as built.

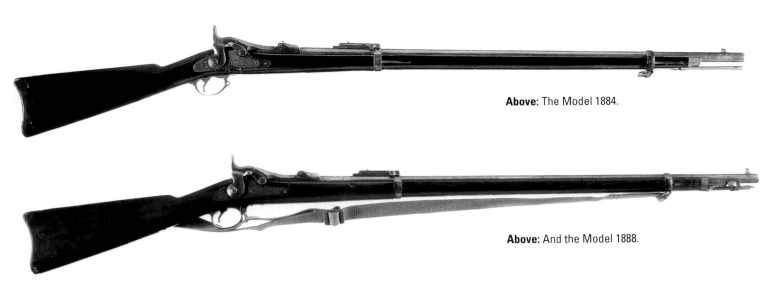

Above: The Model 1884.

Above: And the Model 1888.

Below: A close-up of the rifle with the breech open and a .45-70 round.

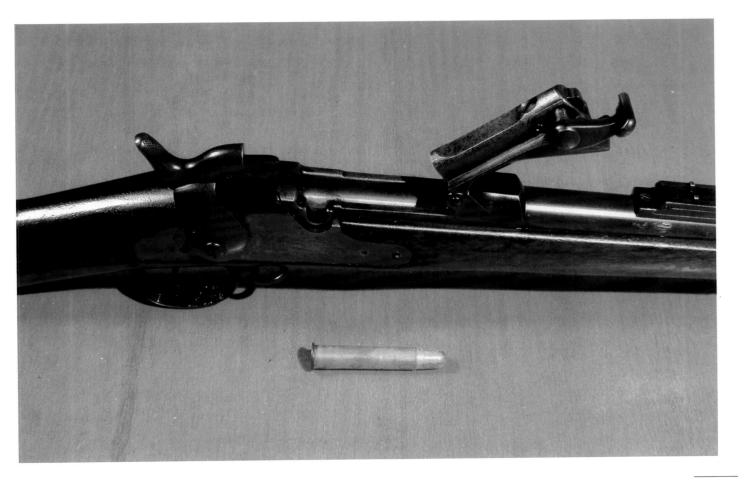

Springfield Model 1879 Carbine

The Model 1873 Cavalry Carbine and its successor the Model 1879 were both made as original Allin trapdoor models. They were also the standard weapons of the U.S. Cavalry in the Indian Wars of the 1870s and 1880s.

Opposite page: A Sergeant of the 6th U.S. Cavalry flanked by Corporal in the 7th Cavalry in Winter Capaign Dress circa 1890, both with Springfield carbines with the Allin Trapdoor action.

Above: Shown here is a very early production example of the original Model 1873.

Above: This one is a saddle-ring version of the Model 1879.

Above: Here we have a particularly fine Model 1879, completed in 1880, which appears to have been neither issued nor fired.

Springfield M1903

Type: Bolt–action magazine fed rifle	
Origin: Springfield Armory, Springfield, Massachusetts	
Caliber: 30-06	
Barrel length: 24 inches	

This was one of the great weapons in the history of the United States. Soon after the introduction of the Krag-Jorgensen rifle in 1894, the U.S. Army began to look at the idea of yet another rifle, this time using the Mauser action. Initially it was planned to have a 30-inch barrel for the infantry and a 20-inch barrel for a cavalry carbine, but this was changed to a universal rifle with a 24-inch barrel, firing the .30-03 round. The new rifle, always known as "the Springfield" from its main place of manufacture, had a Mauser-type bolt and a five-round magazine with a cut-off plate. There were the inevitable changes in the first few years, the most important being the adoption of the .30-06 round with a lighter bullet with a sharper nose, which was introduced in 1906; this had greater muzzle velocity, a low trajectory, increased maximum theoretical range to 2,850 yards, and also reduced the wear on the barrel. New rifles were built chambered for this round, but existing rifles had to be re-chambered, although this was not a difficult task.

The Ml903 proved very popular, proving itself in the trenches of Northern France during WWI, its only significant disadvantage being its small (five round) magazine capacity. It remained in service for many years and underwent many modifications, including the introduction of the Pedersen device in 1918, which gave it an automatic fire capability, and the introduction of a pistol grip to the stock in 1929. The first one shown is a very early production rifle, which was initially chambered for the .30-03 round, but had not yet been issued when the .30-06 round was accepted for service and was consequently rechambered.

Opposite page: An American Serviceman kitted out ready to join his colleagues in the trenches of Northern France.

Below: The M 1903 used the well-proven Mauser action and was a popular service weapon.

Here we have an early production M1903 fitted with a 1904-pattern sling. It shows the unmistakable outline of "the Springfield" with its humped handguard, grasping-groove, and straight stock.

A similar, early production version, but with a slightly different pattern rear sight.

This one was produced around 1918 for the Marine Corps, but was later modified by the Corps to take a Sedgely-made barrel.

CALIBER .30 SPRINGFIELD RIFLE

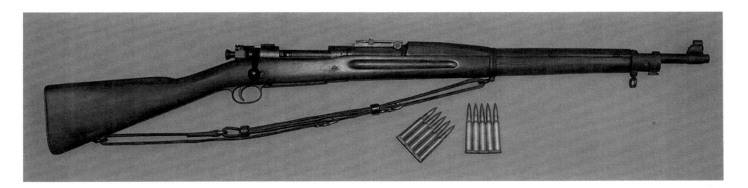

Above: M1903 with the 5 round ammunition clips that fitted the magazine. The small magazine capacity was one of the few downsides of the gun.

Right: Target practice! Note the peep sight.

Model	Produced	Years	Number
M1901	Springfield	1901	100
M1903	Springfield	1903–27	1,275,000
	Rock Island	1904–19	347,000
	Remington	1941–3	348,00
M1903 Mk 1	Remington/		
	Springfield	1918–20	100,000
M1903A1	Springfield	1929–?	100
M1903A3	Remington	1942–44	708,000
	Smith & Corona	1942–44	234,600
M1903A3 National Match	Springfield	1956	850
TOTALS			**1,958,706**

Thompson Submachine Gun

Type: Submachine gun	
Origin: Auto Ordnance Corporation	
Caliber: .45	
Barrel length: 10.5 inches	

Below: Top is the Thompson M1928 and an alternative 50-round drum magazine and below the M1A1 with sling.

Colonel J. T. Thompson developed his Thompson, or "Tommy" gun during the course of World War I, but it arrived too late to be used in action. The Auto-Ordnance Corporation found that submachine guns were difficult to sell during peacetime, especially during the Great Depression. They somewhat surmounted this difficulty by advertising the gun quite heavily. This resulted in small but steady sales to law enforcement agencies, and some of the guns also found their way into the hands of various criminal types. A surprising variety of Thompson models were made. Almost all of these were 0.45-inch caliber and one or two were made as automatic rifles rather than submachine guns. Some examples were also produced in England by the Birmingham Small Arms Company. The M1928A1 version was produced with several minor design changes, was the final peacetime version of the weapon, and was more complex than the M1A1. The gun worked on the usual blowback system. Unusually, the gun also has a delay device to prevent the bolt from opening until the barrel pressure had dropped. Two squared grooves were cut into the sides of the bolt at an angle of 45 degrees, the lower ends being nearer to the

Opposite page: Johnny Depp as John Dillinger in *Public Enemies* carrying the archetypal Thompson.

Opposite page: The American soldier in 1944 (with Thompson) from a set of color posters commemorating the history of the U.S. fighting man.

face of the bolt, and an H-shaped bridge was fitted into these. When the bolt was fully home, the lower ends of the H-piece engaged in recess in the receiver. When the cartridge fired, the pressure was enough to cause it to rise, thus allowing the bolt to go back after a brief delay. From the point of view of safety, this was unnecessary, but had the useful effect of slowing the cyclic rate, which greatly improved its firing accuracy. The gun used either a 50-round drum or a 20-round box magazine.

The real breakthrough for the Thompson submachine gun came in 1938, when the United States Army adopted the weapon. Other contemporary guns were more modern, and some were better weapons, but the Thompson had the supreme advantage of being available. Demand for the gun rose greatly at the outbreak of war. Apart from the domestic needs of the United States, Great Britain also bought as many Thompsons as it was offered from 1940 onwards. Like many other pre-war models, the Thompson had been produced with great attention to detail, but simplification was imperative to accelerate production. The result of this work was the M1, whose main mechanical difference was the abolition of the H-piece and the substitution of a heavier bolt to compensate for this. Externally, the main differences were the absence of the compensator on the muzzle, the substitution of a straight forehand for the forward pistol grip (although this had been optional on the Model 28), the removal of the rather complex backsight, and its replacement by a simple flip. The new gun could not take the 50-round drum. But this had never been entirely reliable in dirty conditions, so it was no great loss. A new 30-round box magazine was introduced and the earlier 20-round magazine also fit the new gun. Yet another simplification, the incorporation of a fixed firing pin on the face of the bolt, resulted in the M1A1 version of the gun. By then, the basic design of the weapon was almost a quarter of a century old, but the Thompson gave excellent service in the critical years between 1939 and 1945. Although it was heavy to carry, the gun was also reliable, and had excellent stopping power.

Right: The M1928 with the 50-round magazine fitted.

Wells Fargo Shotgun

Type: Double-barreled shotgun

Origin: Remington Arms Co., Ilion, New York

Caliber: 12 gauge

Barrel length: 20 inches

Below: The documentation with this Remington Model 1889 certifies that it was shipped to the Wells Fargo company to enable their stagecoach drivers to defend themselves and their cargo and passengers from robbery and attack.

Below right: Wells Fargo inscription above the barrels of the Wells Fargo Remington shotgun.

Wells Fargo was one of the great institutions of the West and was a positive force for the civilizing of the Wild Frontier. Its very name conjures a thrilling image of a six-horse stagecoach loaded with gold, thundering across the romantic plains landscape. In fact, its activities became part of the fabric of the American West, serving people of every background and profession, and actively seeking to control lawlessness. Henry Wells and William Fargo founded the company in 1852, and the company's first office was set up in downtown San Francisco at 420 Montgomery Street, right in the heart of the tent city of the '49ers. The new company offered banking (buying gold, selling bank drafts) and express, secure carriage for all kinds of cargo, especially gold dust and bullion from the newly sunk mines. Right from the beginning, there was also a thread of altruism in the company culture. Wells Fargo offered their services to all "men, women, or children, rich or poor, white or black." Indeed, they ran their business for all the settlers and frontiers people of the West, including blacks, whites, and Spanish-speaking Hispanics. William Wells was also an early proponent of sexual equality, later founding Wells College for Women in New York with the slogan, "Give her the opportunity!" Several women were agents by the 1880s, sometimes taking over from their husbands as company employees when they were widowed. Veterans of the U.S. Army have also worked for the company for over 150 years, helping to build the great overland stage lines and founding the financial service aspect of the company.

Integrity was a great factor in the success of the business and Wells Fargo agents often became highly respected figures in the new towns and volatile mining settlements of the West.

They were recruited from well-respected members of the community, including storekeepers and attorneys, and each was given a certificate of appointment by the company. As well as the Express service, the agents also offered basic banking and financial services.

The company started its overland stagecoach line in the 1860s, and was also partly responsible for the Butterfield Overland Mail Company established in 1858 (which they later took over). They sent the mail by the fastest means possible, stagecoach, steamship, railroad, pony rider, or telegraph, and their operatives often brought the mail through at dreadful personal risk. Wells Fargo also employed

Above: Wells Fargo issued all their operatives with recognizable badges, and their logo became a symbol of civilization moving westwards.

Right: A traditional-style hold up of a Wells Fargo stage.

Above: A sawn-off version of the double barreled shotgun was also used by Wells Fargo for concealing under the drivers seat.

detectives to investigate fraud and any other illegal practices in connection with their business, together with armed escorts and shotgun riders to discourage theft and hold-ups. They were reputed to carry cut-down shotguns, which were easy to conceal under the seat of a wagon and lethal at close range.

Left: Madison Larkin was a Wells Fargo Messenger and shotgun guard, and would have worked for one Wells Fargo local agent. He was photographed at Phoenix in 1877.

Winchester Repeating Shotguns

Type: Tubular magazine lever-action rifle

Origin: Winchester Repeating Arms Co., New Haven, Connecticut

Caliber: .44 Henry

Barrel length: see text

For over 200 years the shotgun as a weapon had been restricted to firing a maximum of two shots. Colt's revolving shotgun had not proved a success as it was too bulky when fully loaded. Thus the traditional "side by side" configuration had endured.

American gun inventor John M Browning challenged the status quo when he developed a series of repeating shotguns starting with what became the Winchester Model 1887 lever-action shotgun. Winchester bought most of Browning's patents at this time, the Model 1897 being no exception.

Above: Winchester Model 1887 lever-action shotgun

John Browning's interest was never confined to one type of weapon nor to one method of operation, and with his lever-action shotgun successfully launched he turned to a new action, which led to a new design, patented under U.S. 441, 390/1890. Again it was sold to Winchester, who put it on the market in 1894 as the Model 1893. Like the lever-action weapon, this had a tubular magazine under the barrel, but this time it was operated by a sliding forearm, usually referred to as pump action or slide action, but also sometimes called trombone action. It was made in 12-gauge only, with a five-round magazine (plus one in the chamber), top ejection, and either 30-inch or 32-inch barrels. It was in production for only three years and was then replaced by the Model 1897.

Below: Winchester Model 1893 pump-action shotgun

The Model 1897 was a modified version of the Model 1893, which could be taken down for storage and transportation. It had a longer chamber, side ejection, and improved stock and was built around a more robust frame than the Model 1893. It achieved great popularity in the United States and the standard version remained in production until 1957—an astonishing 60 years, thus making it one of the great guns of America. The Model 1897 was an immediate success with sportsmen and law enforcers and breakers alike as it was a formidable weapon. Devil Anse Hatfield of feuding Hatfields & McCoys fame had one.

There were at least eight versions. The Standard, Trap, Pigeon, and Brush were all produced in either 12-gauge (30-inch barrel) or 16-gauge (28-inch barrel), with minor differences according to their intended function. The Brush Gun was also made in a takedown version. The Tournament was made in 12-gauge only with a 30-inch barrel. The Riot Gun was made in 12-gauge, with a 20-inch barrel, and

fired buckshot. The Trench Gun was very similar to the Riot Gun but had a slotted barrel handguard and a bayonet lug. Production years were: Standard 1897–1957; Trap 1897–1931; Special Trap 1932–1939; Pigeon 1897–1939; Brush 1897–1931; Riot 1898–1935; Tournament 1910–1931; Standard Trap 1931–1939 and Trench 1917–1935.

Right: Head of one of the feuding families of the Hatfields and the McCoys, Devil Anse Hatfield poses with his Winchester Model 1897 slide-action shotgun in a "ready to feud" attitude. He also wears two ammunition bandoliers. The lower bandolier is full of Winchester 12 gauge shotgun ammunition while the other contains smaller caliber handgun ammunition, probably for his Colt Bisley revolver.

Left: Texas Ranger "Texas" John Slaughter totes a Model 1897 Winchester pump action shotgun. He wears a bandolier with shotgun shells around his waist and has a pearl handled Colt single-action in his holster. Repeating shotguns were popular with the Rangers.

Winchester Model 1866

Type: Tubular magazine, lever-action rifle/musket/carbine

Origin: Winchester Repeating Arms Company, New Haven, Connecticut

Caliber: .44 Henry

Barrel length: see text

The Model 1860 Henry rifle represented some significant advances, the most important being that the sixteen-round magazine gave the shooter a major increase in firepower. But it also suffered from some drawbacks, several of which had tactical implications. The first was the shooter's forehand held the barrel, which became very hot in a prolonged engagement. The second, and more important, was that the tubular magazine had to be disengaged and reloaded from the front, which meant that the weapon had to be taken out of action and engage the shooter's attention until the task had been completed. Thirdly, the magazine had slots, which allowed dirt to enter.

Right: A group of old timers. The man on the left has a Winchester Model 1866.

The company changed its name from the New Haven Arms Company to the Henry Repeating Rifle Company in 1865 and to the Winchester Repeating Arms Company in 1866. This meant that when these problems were overcome in a new model that was introduced that year, it carried the now legendary name of the "Winchester Model 1866."

The heating problem was overcome very simply—the weapon was fitted with a wooden forearm so that the shooter's hand never came into contact with the barrel. The ammunition solution was simple from the shooter's point-of-view, but more complicated for the engineers because the works foreman at the Winchester factory redesigned the gun so that the magazine tube was fixed and rounds were pushed in through a spring-loaded loading-port at the rear. The result was that the shooter could keep his eye on the battle and hold his weapon in the aiming position with his left hand while reloading with his right. This also meant that the magazine slots were deleted.

The distinctive brass frame gave the gun its nickname the Yellowboy. It was popular with westerners, particularly cowboys and lawmen who found that gun could be easily fired and reloaded on horseback. The saddle-ring Carbine was the most popular in this respect and was the gun made famous by the king of Screen cowboys, John Wayne.

The Model 1866 was in production from 1866 to 1898, during which time some 170,000 were completed. These were split into three main types: carbine, with round barrel (127,000); sporting rifle (28,000) with either round or octagonal

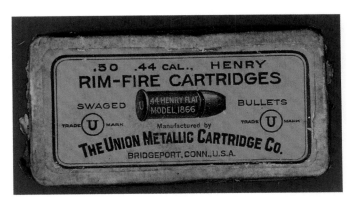

Above: A box of the rim fire cartridges for the Model 1866. These were similar to the ones used by the earlier Henry rifle.

Below: The brass frame gave the gun its nickname the "Yellow boy."

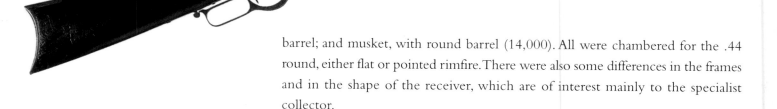

barrel; and musket, with round barrel (14,000). All were chambered for the .44 round, either flat or pointed rimfire. There were also some differences in the frames and in the shape of the receiver, which are of interest mainly to the specialist collector.

Above is a sporting model, made in 1878. It has a 24.4-inch barrel and is chambered for the .44 Henry round. Note the forearm, which solved the hand problem, the color of the brass, which earned the weapon its nickname of "the yellow boy" and the loading gate, which solved the reloading problem.

Below is the saddle-ring carbine, made in 1883, with a 20-inch barrel, which resulted in a shorter magazine, reducing the capacity from seventeen rounds to thirteen. Note the saddle-ring on the left side of the weapon and the company's latter of authenticity, certifying the details of this particular weapon.

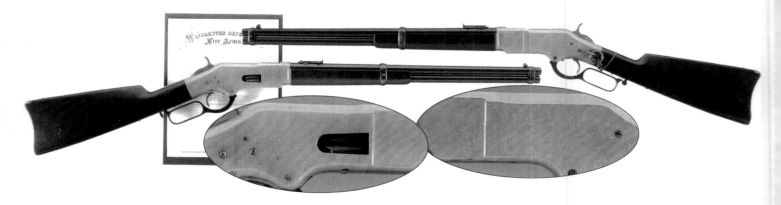

The Model 1866 Musket had a 27-inch round barrel, but unlike the other variations, the seventeen round magazine did not extend to the muzzle. This particular weapon (with bayonet) was sold to a South American army, but after years of hard service there, was declared surplus and returned to the United States.

Opposite: Movie icon John Wayne with his signature Winchester carbine.

Vinchester Model 1873

e: Tubular magazine, lever-
:ion rifle/musket/carbine

gin: Winchester Repeating Arms
mpany, New Haven,
nnecticut

liber: .44-.40

rrel length: see text

e right: Winchester rifles were popular with
nforcement groups like
Texas Rangers.

w: A very early production Model 1873
ng rifle, this was shipped in 1874 and has
number #684. It has the twenty-four-inch
onal barrel. The forearm has an iron cap,
e cover is shown (although this actual
may be a replacement).

The Model 1873 offered three advances over the Model 1866. First, it
a stronger frame, which was originally made of iron, but from 18
was made from steel. Secondly, it had a dust cover over the action. Thirdly
perhaps most important of all, however, was that although other calibers
available, most were chambered for the .44–.40 round, which was the san
that used in the Colt single-action revolver, thus greatly easing the u
logistical problems, particularly in the rigorous environment of the fro
Indeed, the Model 1873 had a thoroughly well-deserved title of "The
That Won The West."

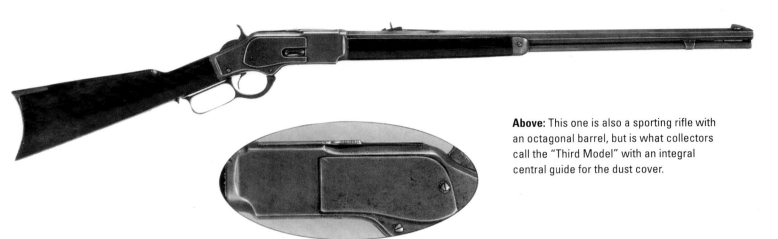

Above: This one is also a sporting rifle with an octagonal barrel, but is what collectors call the "Third Model" with an integral central guide for the dust cover.

Below left: A box of .44-40 ammunition which could be used in the rifle and the Colt 1873 single-action Frontier Model.

Below: John Wayne, again, with his trademark Winchester carbine which was actually a Model 1892 instead of an 1873

The gun reached popular acclaim many years later when it was the subject of a movie, *Winchester '73*, starring James Stewart.

As with the Model 1866, the Model 1873 was sold in three versions: musket with 30-inch round barrel; sporting rifle with 24-inch round, octagonal, or round/octagonal barrel; and carbine with 20-inch round barrel. There are also the usual minor changes over the production run, mainly concerning the dust cover. In 1884, Winchester introduced a new version of the Model 1873 chambered for .22 rimfire, but it did not prove particularly popular, with some 19,000 sold over a twenty-year production run. Overall some 720,000 Model 1873s of all versions had been sold when production ended in 1919.

The Model 1892 was, in essence, an updated Model 1873 employing a slightly smaller version of Browning's Model 1886 action. It was available in five calibers—

Above: A standard Model 1873 saddle-ring carbine with a 20-inch round barrel; it was made in 1889.

Right: A poster for the 1950 movie starring James Stewart celebrating the gun.

Below: A real life cowboy with his Winchester.

.218 Bee, .25-20, .32-20, .38-40 and .44-40—and various barrel lengths appropriate to the caliber; there was also a choice of magazine sizes in some models. There were five variants: Sporting Rifle, Fancy Sporting Rifle, Carbine and Trapper's Carbine and Musket. More than one million Model 1892s were sold, with the production run extending from 1892 to 1932 for most models, and to 1941 for carbines

Above: This one is a late production (1909) Model 1873 Trapper's Carbine with a shortened 16.25-inch round barrel.

Below: This one is the musket version, with a thirty-inch round barrel and the associated 18.5-inch "spike" bayonet—considering its age, this example is in exceptionally good, virtually mint, condition.

Above and left: An exact half-scale miniature in .22 caliber.

Winchester Model 1894

Type: Tubular magazine, lever-action rifle/musket/carbine

Origin: Winchester Repeating Arms Company, New Haven, Connecticut

Caliber: .30-30 smokeless

Barrel length: see text

The Model 1894 was the first Winchester to be designed from the outset to use smokeless powder cartridges and has proved immensely popular; it was the first sporting rifle to exceed one million sales, the total production by 1963 was some two million, and today the figure stands at about seven million. With a production run already in excess of 110 years, it is not surprising that there have been a bewildering number of variations, with the company's catalog listing fourteen on offer in 2005. In general, however, there have been the usual five basic variants: Sporting, Fancy Sporting, Extra Lightweight, Carbine, and Trapper's Carbine.

Right: To hunt whitetail deer requires a gun that is quick to maneuver and fire in the dense woods of the East Coast.

Opposite page: "Little Miss Sureshot" Annie Oakley poses with her Winchester Model 1894.

Above: An early production (serial #102,053; 1897) Model 1894 Sporting Rifle with a 26-inch barrel, chambered for Winchester's smokeless .30-30 cartridge, and a solid frame; it has all the standard features of the time.

Above: An almost identical Sporting Rifle but with a takedown frame

Above: Made in 1910,with a 26-inch .30-.30 octagonal barrel this rifle was used in the 1970s as the base for a remarkable exercise in the art of engraving by Angelo Bee. There is heavy scroll engraving on virtually all surfaces, with a vignette of two dogs and a bear on the left side and of a moose on the right, all inlaid with gold. All outlines, borders, and most lettering are also inlaid with gold. Of equal merit are the forearm and stock, both in Turkish Circassian , walnut, which were checkered and carved in oak-leaf style by Angelo's wife, Maria.

The Model 1894 was compact and lightweight, yet packed a considerable punch. It was easy to carry and had a strong ergonomic appeal, which made it popular with hunters. Its quick shooting abilities made it ideal for shooting game such as white tailed deer whose habitat is the dense forests of the Eastern states. Here most kills have to be made at relatively short notice and distances. Because of these qualities, it was the first sporting rifle to sell over 7,000,000 units. The millionth Model 1894 was given to President Calvin Coolidge in 1927, the one-and-a-half-millionth rifle to President Harry S. Truman on May 8, 1948, and the two-millionth unit to President Dwight D. Eisenhower in 1953.

Below: A number of carbines were supplied to Canada, as was this example, chambered for .30-30. The carbine is still accompanied by the brassard of the 124th Company of the Pacific Coast Militia Regiment, which patrolled Canada's West coast against Japanese incursions in World War Two.

Opposite page: Theodore Roosevelt in buckskin garb with his lightweight Model 1876. This gun was a transition between the Model 1873 and the 1894 as it used full–power centerfire cartridges.

Winchester Model 1895

Type: Lever-action, box magazine-fed rifle

Origin: Winchester Repeating Arms Co., New Haven, Connecticut

Caliber: .30-30

Barrel length: 28 inches

Right: Theodore Roosevelt on Safari in Africa with the gun and a Rhino.

Opposite page: Roosevelt was so enamored with the Model 1895 that he personally equipped his Rough Riders with the rifles at the outset of the Spanish-American War. The Rough Riders (the 1st United States Volunteer Cavalry) was one of three volunteer regiments raised in 1898, at a time when the U.S. Army was still suffering from a manpower shortage in the wake of the Civil War a mere thirty years earlier. The term was a popular one, borrowed from Buffalo Bill, who described his Wild West show as a "congress of Rough Riders."

Below: A very early production Model 1895 with the flat-sided receiver, which characterizes the first 5,000 (actual serial of this weapon is #3797). It has a 28-inch .30-.30 caliber barrel and clearly shows the unmistakable profile created by the integral magazine.

John Browning's Model 1895 was the first Winchester lever-action to feature a box magazine, in this case a non-detachable type with a five-round capacity. It was designed to meet the requirements of the new high-power smokeless cartridge then becoming available and was made in nine calibers. It received the highest possible endorsement when it was adopted by Theodore Roosevelt as his favorite hunting rifle. Some 426,000 were produced between 1895 and 1931.

As with previous models, it was produced in Sporting Rifle, Fancy Sporting Rifle, Carbine, and Musket variants, with some interesting examples in the latter category. The U.S. Army purchased a number chambered for the .30-40

Top: Another Model 1895 Rifle, in this case chambered for the British government .303 cartridge (although this is not a military weapon). It has a 28-inch round barrel and a Lyman sight mounted on the receiver

Above: A musket version supplied to the U.S. Army in 1898, with a 28-inch barrel and chambered for .30-.40.

Krag round for use in the Spanish-American war, while the Imperial Russian Army bought some 290,000 in 1915-16. Other versions of the Model 1895 Musket were produced for use in NRA competition shooting.

The Zouave Rifle

Type: Muzzle-loading, percussion rifle	
Origin: E. Remington and Sons, Ilion, New York	
Caliber: .58	
Barrel length: 33 inches	

The name Zouave originated in the French Army. These troops were first raised in Algeria in 1831 with one and later two battalions, initially recruited solely from the Zouaoua, a tribe of Berbers. They were characterized by loose baggy pantaloons, a fez with a colored tassel (usually yellow, blue, green, or red) and turban, a tight-fitting short jacket (some without buttons), a wide 10-foot-long sash, white leggings, and a short leather cuff for the calf, called jambieres. The sash was especially difficult to put on, often requiring the help of another Zouave. This outfit was better suited for warm climates and rough terrain. The loose pantaloons allowed for greater freedom of movement than trousers, while the short jacket was much cooler than the long wool blouse worn by most armies of the time. The Zouave uniform was, in fact, sometimes too elaborate, to the extent of being unwieldy.

Numerous Zouave regiments were organized at the outset of the Civil War by soldiers of both sides who adopted the name and the North African–inspired uniforms. The Union army had more than 70 volunteer Zouave regiments throughout the conflict, while the Confederates fielded about 25 Zouave companies. A feature of the American Zouave units, at least in the opening stages of the Civil War, was the light infantry tactics and drill they employed. Traditionally Zouaves used light infantry tactics that emphasised open-order formations, with several feet between soldiers, rather than the customary close order, with its characteristic "touch of elbows." They moved at double time, rather than marching at a stately cadence, and they lay on their backs to load their rifles rather than standing to do so. To fire, they rolled prone and sometimes rose on one knee. Arguably the most famous Union Zouave regiments were from New York and Pennsylvania: the 5th New York Volunteer Infantry, "Duryee's Zouaves" (after its first colonel, Abram Duryee), the 114th Pennsylvania Infantry; "Collis's Zouaves" (after their colonel, Charles H. T.

Below: The Remington Model 1863 was a pretty gun with brass furniture and ergonomic proportions

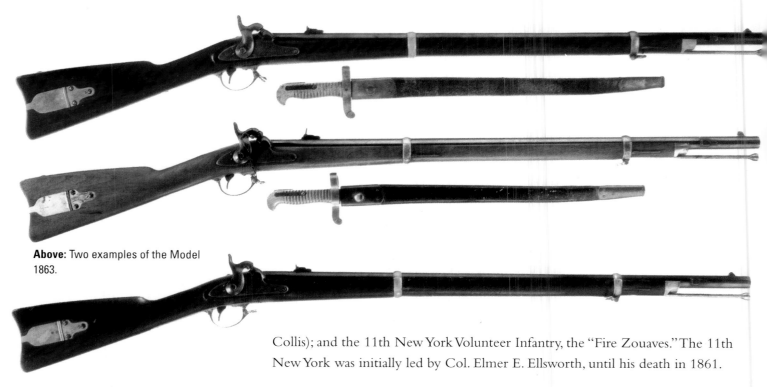

Above: Two examples of the Model 1863.

Below: Two examples of locks from the gun.

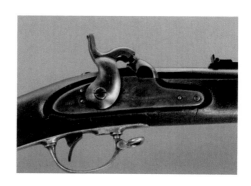

Collis); and the 11th New York Volunteer Infantry, the "Fire Zouaves." The 11th New York was initially led by Col. Elmer E. Ellsworth, until his death in 1861.

The name Zouave was also given to a famous rifle, the Remington Model 1863. On July 30th, 1861, the Ordnance Department asked E. Remington & Sons to manufacture "10,000 stands of arms, .58 inch caliber, and to have three-leaf rear sight and a cupped ramrod, with sword bayonet stud similar to those of the Harpers Ferry rifle model of 1855." This order arrived in Ilion during the funeral of Eliphalet Remington. Despite the sad times, the Remington brothers accepted the government's order, but were unable to deliver any rifles, as their machinery was tied up with fulfilling revolver contracts. When the Remington brothers saw that they were in danger of default, they requested a contract extension, which was granted. On August 11, 1862, this contract was re-issued for 10,000 Harpers Ferry pattern rifles with sword bayonets, caliber .58—all furnished with regular appendages—and packed 20 rifles and appendages in each box—at a cost of $17 for each arm, complete.

Remington acquired the machinery for the large job, and contracted with Collins & Co. to supply the sword bayonets and scabbards. The first delivery of 500 finished rifles and bayonets was made on April 18, 1863, and deliveries continued at a rate of one thousand rifles per month. In all 7,501 rifles were delivered on this contract before it expired.

On December 13, 1863, Remington was awarded yet another contract for Harpers Ferry rifles—this one for 2,500 rifles and bayonets at $17 for each arm, complete, with deliveries to be completed by January 8, 1864. All 2,500 rifles, including many second-class arms, were delivered between December 23, 1863, and January 8, 1864.

Present-day collectors refer to these contract rifles as Remington Zouave rifles, not Harpers Ferry rifles. Similar to the standard Model 1863, it was slightly shorter and had only two barrel bands. It's not known with any certainty why the name "Zouave" was given to this weapon, as there are no records to suggest it was issued particularly to these regiments with their unusual colorful clothing. As can be seen from the examples we show, many surviving Zouave rifles are in excellent condition, and it appears that many didn't see hard active service.

Below: These men of the 4th Michigan Infantry display the unusual and often brightly colored Zouave uniforms that some units wore. As well as their rifles, they also have Colt Army revolvers tucked into their waistbands.

Index

Acknowledgments

The publishers gratefully acknowledge the invaluable assistance by various organizations and individual collectors with photographs appearing in this book:

Patrick M. Hogan, Rock Island Auction Co.Moline, Illinois.

Paintings by Don Troiani www.historicalartprints.

Patrick Reardon for allowing us to photograph his civil war collection.

The National Archive.

M.P.T.V. Images, Van Nuys, California.